# ABOUT THE AUTHOR

Jan Roberts has spent more than 40 years in the healthcare industry, 30 of them working in the area of women's reproductive health. She has an Honours degree in Pharmacy from the University of Sydney and a Postgraduate Diploma in Clinical Nutrition. For more than two decades she has presented seminars and keynote addresses to health professionals, students and prospective parents throughout Australia, New Zealand and the United States. She contributes regularly to various magazines and professional journals and is also a successful entrepreneur, developing and marketing products and services that support her vision for a healthier, happier next generation. In 2010 she was short-listed for the Vodafone World of Difference Award and in 2011 received the University of Sydney's Pharmacy Alumni Award for Achievement. She is the co-author with Francesca Naish of the bestselling Better Babies series, also published by Random House.

**Also by Jan Roberts**
*Healthy Parents, Healthy Baby*

**Also by Francesca Naish and Jan Roberts**
*The Natural Way to Better Babies*
*The Natural Way to a Better Pregnancy*
*The Natural Way to Better Birth and Bonding*
*The Natural Way to Better Breastfeeding*

# Healthy Parents, Healthy Toddler

## A GUIDE TO BONDING, BREASTFEEDING
## AND THE TODDLER YEARS

### JAN ROBERTS

Doubleday

A Doubleday book
Published by Random House Australia Pty Ltd
Level 3, 100 Pacific Highway, North Sydney NSW 2060
www.randomhouse.com.au

First published by Doubleday in 2012

'In your kitchen' recipes reproduced with kind permission from Pauline and
David Nemeth.

Addresses for companies within the Random House Group can be found at
www.randomhouse.com.au/offices

National Library of Australia
Cataloguing-in-Publication Entry

Roberts, Jan.

Healthy parents, healthy toddler / Jan Roberts.

ISBN 978 1 74275 220 4 (pbk.)

Parenting – Health aspects.
Parent and child – Health aspects.
Motherhood – Health aspects.
Natural childbirth.
Child rearing.

649.1

Cover photograph © Valentin Casarsa /iStockphoto
Cover design by Christabella Designs
Internal design by Christabella Designs
Typeset in Sabon 11/17 pt by Midland Typesetters, Australia
Printed in Australia by Griffin Press, an accredited ISO AS/NZS 14001:2004
Environmental Management System printer

Random House Australia uses papers that are natural, renewable and recyclable
products and made from wood grown in sustainable forests. The logging and
manufacturing processes are expected to conform to the environmental regulations
of the country of origin.

*For Mikey – he knows why.*

# CONTENTS

# NOTE TO READERS

In this book I refer to many self-help and some practitioner-guided treatments. If you are in any doubt about what you should do on your own or what requires professional assistance, be sure to seek help. When consulting health professionals, find ones who will support your desire for a natural approach to labour, who are knowledgeable about breastfeeding matters (e.g., a lactation consultant or breast-feeding counsellor) and finally who will offer natural medicines before pharmaceuticals for your family.

Some of the nutritional supplements and nutraceuticals that I recommend are available from holistic and natural health practitioners and selected health food stores and pharmacies. If not, they are all readily available from Jan's Picks on my website, www.flurishh.com. I have provided guidelines regarding general use, but always follow the dosage insert. There are risks involved in over-supplementing. If you have any specific concerns, you should consult a natural health practitioner.

Finally, throughout this book, you'll find your baby referred to as 'he'. Indulge me – it's not a preference for male babies but rather a convention that I find easier to use in order to distinguish between mother and baby. Definitely no discrimination or sexism intended!

# A FEW WORDS
# FROM JAN . . .

As parents today, you have some extraordinary challenges ahead of you. First of all, you have to navigate the minefield of the medically managed reproductive cycle. At every step, from conception, through pregnancy, to birth and breastfeeding and beyond, you'll be offered solutions that medical science has developed. Many of your friends may opt for those solutions. You may be convinced that what man created, supervised, rearranged or manipulated is at least equivalent, if not preferable, to what Nature designed. It can be very difficult to move beyond the orthodox medical dogma to follow a natural path and at no time is that more challenging than during your parenting journey when what is 'best' for your precious baby is the experts' all-powerful trump card!

If you successfully negotiate your way through the maze to enjoy a conscious conception, a healthy pregnancy, a natural birth and a long-term breastfeeding relationship, you're not out of the woods yet, even though you're certainly off to a flying start! You then have to nurture your child's interaction with the world, rather than restrict it – at a time when the world is often seen as an unsafe and threatening place. You need to foster your child's inquisitiveness and aid his explorations, rather than limit them – at a time when you may be preoccupied with your own relationship, business or career, also at a time when your child may want to explore no further than the nearest electronic medium. You are asked to follow the plan that Nature devised for his optimal physical, mental and emotional development – at a time when you may have little idea of what that plan entails.

Having negotiated my own way through the maze and now looking back at a job pretty well done, I'd like to share something of that journey. Moved by what I've referred to in the past as 'the line of least resistance', today I would describe my decisions and choices a little differently. With new and exciting research showing the importance (particularly during your parenting journey) of aligning the gut, heart and cerebral brains (more in coming chapters), I now know that unwittingly, I was trying to do just that.

Of course my family – bearing in mind that your nearest and dearest can be your greatest critics but also your greatest teachers – describe my parenting style another way. They see me simply as 'Slack Alice', a reference to the character created by a famous British stand-up comic of the 1970s. The nickname, originally bestowed on me in 1973 by my brother-in-law when we shared a campervan and a road trip across the United States, has stuck. At the time it was assigned in direct juxtaposition to my sister's nickname which was 'Mrs Whisk'.

My ability to ignore the campervan's dusty floor when there was a book to be read in the sunshine or a glass of wine to be enjoyed by a campfire translated well to mothering. Lots of my choices were simply the alternative to something I saw as a much less appealing option. Now I'm more aware of how decisions are usually made, often ignoring a sense of 'rightness' in the gut or an 'emotion' that tugs at the heart strings, accepting and following expert advice that is directed solely to, and run exclusively by, the logical, rational left brain.

Looking back at the early days of my own parenting journey, I can only say I was extraordinarily fortunate that something deep-seated and 'right' sang out to me and that I listened. Ironically, through listening and observing how different my experience of mothering was from that of many others, I set off on the road to creating the book that you now hold in your hand.

So this is how I saw some of the situations that confronted me back in 1984 as a very late-starting, inexperienced, but questioning, first-time mum . . .

- Preconception care? 'At 37, I know a lot of my friends think I've missed the baby-making boat.'
- Prenatal screening and diagnostics? 'Who needs the worry? I'm absolutely trusting my body's ability to make a healthy baby.'
- Birth at home? 'I stay well clear of hospitals – besides, I'm pregnant, not sick.'
- Family bed? 'Avoid waking and stay warm and horizontal is my night-time mantra.'
- Late solids? 'Special meals, mashing, pureeing – forget it.'
- Prolonged breastfeeding? 'When my baby's teething, sick, injured, frustrated, bored, tired or lonely, I just offer the breast!'
- Vaccination? 'You must be kidding – after all the effort I've made to avoid toxins and build a strong immune system.'

This might all sound a bit flippant, a little glib, but it really seems to me that the man-made answers, the scientific and technological solutions to, or manipulations of, conception, pregnancy, birth and breastfeeding and our children's health have created many more problems than they've solved.

The Healthy Parents, Healthy Baby Program, which is contained in this and my previous book, *Healthy Parents, Healthy Baby*, is based on two fundamental principles. First of all, Nature provides an extraordinarily successful blueprint for the healthiest possible conception, gestation, birthing and nurturing of children. Second, the whole reproductive cycle unfolds as Nature intended when it begins with two optimally healthy partners, is fully supported by an abundance of all the nutritional building blocks and takes place in the absence of anything that is potentially toxic.

It helps if you can keep the following in mind:

- Children have no wants, only needs. As parents you will do best when you attend to those needs rather than suppress them, ignore them or view them as selfish manipulation.
- Children come into the world with potential abilities that far exceed those of any other creature. You will be most effective when you truly believe in and foster those abilities, whatever they may be and however far removed from what you imagined or planned for your child.
- Children are driven from within to perfect themselves. You are simply required to recognise the value of that drive rather than see it as something sent to drive *you* to distraction.
- Children are the experts when it comes to being children, and hard as it may sometimes be, you must simply believe in your child's innate wisdom.

If I were to sum it all up in one phrase, I could do no better than quote the words of Maria Montessori, who said, 'Always follow the child.' This message has become the guiding principle of the world-renowned Montessori method of childhood development and education.

In a somewhat different context, I'm calling on the mums (and dads) of the world to join the movement to a wiser, more attached and connected style of parenting, because I think you've drawn the short straw. Parenting was never meant to be so difficult, never meant to be such a labyrinth of procedures and processes, uncertainty and doubt, information and misinformation. The physical, mental and emotional health of your child is in your own hands – not in the hands of doctors, nurses, child psychologists, teachers or any other professional of whatever persuasion. You can give your child the wonderful beginning that is every child's birthright and when you do, there are positive benefits for your family, and even your immediate community, society as a whole and this fabulous blue-green planet on which we live.

Now here's all the 'stuff' you need to know and do, which starts with your preparation for a natural unmedicated birth, takes you through the breastfeeding period and then the early years with your toddler. I also strongly recommend my first book, *Healthy Parents, Healthy Baby*. There you'll find the details of all the things you need to do – covering diet and supplements, exercise, your mental and emotional state and your lifestyle and environment – which apply in equal measure whether you're planning or trying to conceive, pregnant, preparing for the birth of your child, breastfeeding or raising your family.

## The website, game and online shop

But there's still more! These books and ebooks are fully supported by digital elements. The *flurishh* website, www.flurishh.com, is another helpful resource with a forum where you can share your thoughts and experiences with other pregnant couples and new mums and dads – a great way to find support for your own parenting journey. The portal also offers something special in terms of sharing this type of healthcare information – the *flurishh* game. We've created learning situations that require you to actively participate in both the virtual and real worlds. The game is designed to provide preconception, pregnancy and breastfeeding teaching points that are easy to understand and assimilate, together with activities that stimulate learning in a format that is appealing to a new generation of prospective parents. You can play the game on the *flurishh* site or directly through Facebook, at http://apps.facebook.com/flurishh.

My website has an additional section – Jan's Picks. Rather than list a plethora of contacts and resources as in the past, this time I've done the work for you, with the products I refer to throughout the book available from the online shop. They're the best ones to support your efforts to have the healthiest possible pregnancy, breastfeeding relationship and beyond. Each one leads its category and has earned my endorsement because of its role in my own and my family's continuing good health!

So get reading, get playing and get in contact with other mums and dads. It's never too soon (or too late) to embrace the Healthy Parents Program.

## Your Healthy Parents, Healthy Toddler checklist

✓ Natural birth with sympathetic birth attendants
✓ Early bonding
✓ No separation of baby
✓ Immediate breastfeeding
✓ Ongoing nursing on demand
✓ Co-sleeping/family bed
✓ Attention to all your baby's cries
✓ Baby wearing
✓ Baby massage
✓ Exposure to constant movement
✓ Stimulation of all senses
✓ Many and varied experiences (music, reading, conversations)
✓ Strong immune system without vaccination
✓ Solids when baby reaches for food
✓ Healthy food from healthy soil
✓ Family meals
✓ Role models for positive eating habits

✓ Clean/green environment
✓ Prolonged breastfeeding
✓ Infant-led weaning
✓ Exercise as a family
✓ Lots of time in the outdoors
✓ Regular exposure to sunshine
✓ Unstructured playtime
✓ Firm boundaries
✓ Schooling that 'follows the child'
✓ Unequivocal support for your child's interests
✓ Full-time mothering (or fathering) for the first two years
✓ Absolute faith in the benefits of all of the foregoing!

Now read on for all the details . . .

# PART 1:

Welcoming your new baby

# CHAPTER 1

## The best of birth and bonding

### 1. Why natural is better

Giving birth as Nature intended has wonderful benefits for the whole family – benefits that can last a lifetime – and it is an empowering and transformative life event when it occurs the way Nature intended.

### 2. Where?

The debate isn't really about where – you can have a completely natural birth in a conventional labour ward, but if so, choose your hospital carefully.

### 3. With whom?

Choose sympathetic birth attendants and ensure they are aware of your plan and your desire for a natural birth.

### 4. The unexpected

You may have a clear birth plan, calm surroundings, nurturing birth attendants – but sometimes things don't go according to plan.

### 5. Better birth in your hands – good nutrition

We have the evidence – consumption of refined foods reduces the ease of the birthing process.

## 6. Better birth in your hands – the right exercise

Labour is aptly named – it's a work-out! But it will be shorter and easier if you've exercised regularly.

## 7. Better birth in your hands – natural remedies

Optimal nutrition, regular exercise and feeling familiar with your support people and surroundings are all important, but there are some physical things and natural remedies that you can also consider in your preparation for a natural birth.

## 8. What you'll need

Here's a starting point for your list of must-haves and maybe-haves for the birth and for the days that follow.

# 1. Why natural is better

Giving birth as Nature intended has wonderful benefits for the whole family – benefits that can last a lifetime – and it is an empowering and transformative life event. A natural, unmedicated birth has physical, mental and emotional benefits for you, your baby and for other family members. Ensuring the healthiest possible mother and baby means the very important bonding process isn't interrupted and that this long-lasting love affair gets off to a great start.

If you follow all my recommendations from before conception and during pregnancy, you can improve your chances of having that natural birth and the best of bonding too. Give your body all the building blocks it needs to ensure a full-term pregnancy, efficient uterine contractions and optimal production of endorphins and hormones for birth and beyond. Take all the steps to encourage a truly healthy baby, one who will be an active participant in the birth process. Find out all you can about the variations of labour and birth without medication or intervention, gain confidence in your body's innate wisdom and nurture a firm belief in your ability to bring a baby into the world without outside interference. Be aware of the importance of those hours immediately following the birth for optimal bonding.

An important reminder about the current schedule of prenatal screening and diagnostics, which can set you up to rely on medical intervention such as inductions and epidurals at the birth of your baby: if your pregnancy is progressing normally, think hard before you line up for routine ultrasounds or more invasive testing. Keep in mind that these tests were originally designed for use in high-risk pregnancies. Read *Healthy Parents, Healthy Baby* for the mostly ignored downsides of prenatal testing – over-reliance on technology isn't the only negative aspect.

## Benefits of a natural birth – for you and your baby

Given that such a large percentage of women today either voluntarily opt for or finish up with a medicalised birth, what are the advantages of doing it all the natural way? Here's the story in a nutshell . . .

When you labour in a familiar environment, surrounded by the people you know and trust, you'll feel safe and secure. You'll be free of the adrenaline and cortisol surge that will occur during a drive to hospital, be furthered by the stress of admission, increased by an examination of your progress and topped up by other hospital procedures such as connection to monitors or worse.

'So what?' you might ask – that's the story for most women.

Well, the production of the stress hormone adrenaline slows and weakens uterine contractions. There's a very simple reason why so many women turn up at hospital experiencing strong, regular contractions, then find they fade away on admission and are advised to go back home. More stress and less efficient contractions follow until finally back at the hospital a little 'assistance' in the form of a synthetic version of the hormone oxytocin will be applied to get things moving and the downhill slide gathers momentum.

In April 2012, American scientists at the National Institute of Child Health and Human Development published some relevant findings. They compared 39,491 births from 1959 to 1966 with 98,359 births from 2002 to 2008 and identified older maternal age, increased body weight along with *more intrusive obstetric practices* as reasons for women having longer labours than they did 50 years ago.

In a familiar and nurturing environment, however, your contractions stay strong and effective. When you're free to move you'll instinctively adopt the most comfortable positions – the ones that encourage your baby's passage down the birth canal. Labouring naturally, helped by the groaning that comes from down low in your belly, your body produces endorphins, the opioid-like substances that assist you to deal with the pain. While nothing can ever fully prepare a first-time mum for what labour is actually like, some knowledge of what to expect at each stage can give you confidence in the 'knowing' and strength of your body. In short, the most productive support for a labouring woman is appropriate encouragement, physical contact and comfort from massage, hot packs and a warm bath or shower.

In most cases, it can be as simple and straightforward as that. If you're wondering why it isn't that way for so many of your friends and acquaintances, rest assured that by optimising your nutritional status, practising those stretching or yoga poses during your pregnancy, learning how to reduce stress and all you can about the natural birthing process and then, when the time comes, trusting it and going with it, your experience can be very different from theirs. Actively giving birth to your baby in the way that Nature intended is a profound and powerful experience. There is no doubt that it is challenging, but ultimately hugely rewarding and enriching. Author Sheila Kitzinger, writing in *Birth Your Way*, puts it well: 'To carry a child in your body, to make choices between alternatives, to give birth . . . is not a medical event. It is a major life transition.'

Not surprisingly Nature designed the birth process to work simply and efficiently, and for you to be transformed by the experience. When you're feeling empowered and full of a sense of achievement your new life as a mum is off to a head start! This feeling of power and confidence in yourself gives you a firm base for coping with the challenges of mothering that lie ahead. The trust you've gained in your body and your belief in the rightness of letting Nature take its course set strong foundations for following a natural path through feeding and nurturing your baby and parenting your children.

If you're looking for more information, there are plenty of books available, including *The Natural Way to Better Birth and Bonding* which I co-authored with Francesca Naish. In that title, we describe in detail every stage of labour, birth and the early hours and days with your new baby. We also consider the potential downsides of all the possible interventions and show the exercises and yoga poses that you can practise in advance to facilitate an active and natural birth.

There are multiple benefits for a baby who makes his own way into the world. When labour begins, your baby is usually in a head-down position and there's nothing passive or inert about him as he readies himself to be born. A healthy baby is very much part of the process; he's absolutely integral to the progress of your labour and will actually wriggle into the optimum position for his journey down the birth canal, bracing himself against the top of your uterus to do so. His head presses down and together his weight and his vertical position help your cervix to open. Just remember that these natural responses are very much diminished if you're lying in a horizontal position (as your baby will be pushing against gravity) or if you're given any drugs which can interfere with the natural progression of labour.

When your baby makes his entrance into the world under his own steam, he's primed for life outside the womb. That journey is probably one of the most important of his life, because it's been perfectly designed to kickstart all of his vital functions as he begins his (almost) independent existence. At birth he'll be fully alert, he can breastfeed as soon as he's ready and during those first precious hours you'll fall in love with your baby in a way that simply doesn't happen if your birth has been medically managed. That's the long and the short of it. Without the downsides of synthetic induction, an epidural or the major dampening effects of pain-killing drugs or a caesarean section, what follows will now unfold to best advantage. Your baby's arrival without drugs or intervention means you can nurse him straight-away, which heightens your feelings of achievement and fulfilment.

Writing this now, I am transported back through more than two decades to the birth of my own babies and can say wholeheartedly that they remain with me as two extraordinary high points in my life.

# Bonding with your baby

Bonding means falling in love with your baby. Nature has perfected an amazingly effective scheme to ensure your child's survival, to make sure that you will protect and care for him, nurture and provide for him, through thick and thin, feast and famine. This will be the beginning of a powerful, enduring bond with a child that will undoubtedly test your resolve, your patience and your love in the years ahead, and that bond gets off to a flying start following a natural vaginal birth. Of course, that's not to say it can't or won't happen if your early hours with your newborn aren't the ideal I've just described – but it's optimal when you can make the best of Nature's clever plan.

After a natural, unmedicated birth you'll do what all new mothers do instinctively and in a remarkably similar manner: you'll gaze into your baby's eyes, caress, touch, stroke and then nurse him. The baby placed on your chest will make his own way to your nipple, which is the start of some very strong mother–baby interactions. So keep your baby close, even if the hospital staff are itching to wash, weigh and otherwise interfere, and let him nurse as frequently as he wants. Don't let him go!

The skin-on-skin contact from the moment of birth, unlimited nursing, stroking and caressing set you up for a lifetime of positive responses. Your well-bonded baby is more likely to thrive, he'll have fewer health problems and, believe it or not, will probably reach his developmental milestones ahead of less well-bonded children. Incredible what those hormones and feel-good neurotransmitters can achieve!

When you and your baby are well bonded, you're more likely to continue with your breastfeeding relationship. Prolonged breast-feeding will confer a host of benefits that include a greater level of patience and tolerance, directed to both your baby and towards monotony, and even a more nurturing manner of speaking to your child! Since these are all two-way exchanges, your baby will respond accordingly. Your attitude and his response establish a cycle of positive reinforcement that extends well beyond the period following his birth. Read more about this wonderful interaction in Part 2, 'Life with your toddler and beyond'.

Here are some guidelines that can encourage optimal bonding:

✓ Promote oxytocin production during pregnancy through good-quality protein, great sex, lots of cuddles, closeness and regular massage – see *Healthy Parents, Healthy Baby* for all the details.

✓ Make sure your nutritional status is adequate. (Zinc and manganese are particularly important nutrients – both are involved in the formation of hormones that underlie maternal instinct.)

✓ Ensure that the room in which you give birth is warm and the lights are dim.

✓ Let your baby make his own way to your nipple after the birth.

✓ Nurse your baby as soon as he's ready.

✓ Don't let him be taken from you for any reason – weighing, washing and measuring can wait.

✓ Keep him beside you at all times and let him nurse freely and often.

✓ Bonding is enhanced if you're both able to have unlimited skin-on-skin contact – particularly if this is your first baby.

✓ At every opportunity, hold him, touch him, caress and stroke him.

✓ Carry him close to your body in a sling.

✓ Sleep with your baby – apart from boosting your milk supply, it's the best solution to those night-time feeds.

## Preparing yourself

If the recommendations above don't align with the experience of any of your girlfriends, you should make contact with women who know exactly what it's like. Find out everything you can about the normal birth and bonding process. Being well informed and prepared is crucial. Once, this was easy because all babies were born at home, all women had seen other women in labour and close female friends and relatives were there to offer support and assistance. Today, without first-hand experience, you need other sources of information.

Read books that question the routine medical management of birth. Learn what to expect in a normal labour and birth. Find out about obstetrical interventions too. Documentaries of women giving birth may be more valuable than books, since they can convey a realistic picture of the actual experience. Compare women having a completely natural labour and birth with those having a medically managed birth in a hospital setting. Internet forums can be another source of first-hand information, as are accounts of natural unmedicated births in homebirth journals. You need this affirmation of the normality of the process as well as hearing about the wonder and excitement that goes with it.

As I wrote in *Healthy Parents, Healthy Baby*, joining the 'pregnancy club' leaves you at the mercy of those with a high-drama story to share. These folk show little regard for the negative impact they might have and their tales are to be avoided – make sure you associate with positive and supportive people. This is particularly important if you're doing your best to put behind you a previous experience that was less than ideal. If the story-teller persists in telling an alarming tale, you might quieten them by affirming your belief in the ability of your body to do the job it was designed for, and that you prefer to focus on your positive preparation rather than another's negative experiences.

I'll always remember the first meeting I ever attended of my local Nursing Mothers Group (now the Australian Breastfeeding Association). Dave, my firstborn (at home, of course), was about ten weeks old and I was still on the huge emotional high that I'd been on since the moment I held him in my arms. The sad thing was, I was alone in my experience. I couldn't help but think how blessed my whole family had been. More to the point, I was very glad that during my pregnancy I hadn't been exposed to stories like those I was now hearing.

It's pleasing to see that supermodel Gisele Bündchen embraces the same positive attitude. In March 2011 *The Irish Independent News* reported that Bündchen gave birth at home to baby Benjamin. 'Not for one second did it cross my mind that I was not going to have my baby at home,' she said. 'I am not the first person to give birth naturally. Billions of other women have come before me.'

## DID YOU KNOW?

Associate Professor of Midwifery at the University of Western Sydney and media spokesperson for the Australian College of Midwives Hannah Dahlen said babies born vaginally had the advantage of hormonal surges during labour, which made them more wide-eyed and able to connect with their mothers.

## 2. Where?

The debate isn't really about where – you can have a completely natural birth in a conventional labour ward, but if so, choose your hospital carefully.

When deciding where to give birth – at home, at a birth centre or in a hospital – it's really about your attendants and carers being sympathetic to your desire to stay upright, keep moving, change positions and to avoid any form of medical intervention. But when you're making your decision, you also need to keep in mind that things might not go according to plan. You'll have to consider the possibility of an unexpected outcome and who will be present. Following are some of the factors you'll need to take into account.

## At home

A homebirth usually takes place in the presence of a midwife. It gives you complete freedom to do what you please and the best possible chance to have the experience that you want. But it should only be an option if you're absolutely comfortable with the normality of the birthing process and have complete faith in your body's ability to do the work as Nature intended. If you have any niggling doubts or if there are any risk factors, such as a medical condition or pregnancy complication, consider the options that will give you the comfort and security of a backup team in the next room.

## At a birth centre

If you choose to have your baby in a birth centre, you'll develop a relationship with the centre midwives during your antenatal visits. The environment is close to what you would have at home, and you'll be free to move around, to change position, to have your chosen attendants (including your children) present and many of the midwives will be familiar with natural methods of pain relief. And of course, all the technology and the facilities of a hospital are just next door should you need them.

## In a hospital

If you're confident that you can have the birth you want in a full medical setting, if you're seduced by the home-like fittings and fixtures in the maternity suites, the calming colours and the mood lighting and feel you could labour comfortably in this environment, take a close look at their birth statistics before you sign up.

Figures published in 2011 in Australia showed that the induction rates at private hospitals were generally higher than in the public system and rates for C-sections were dramatically higher. This was especially the case for younger, first-time mothers, with caesarean rates reaching a staggeringly high 40 per cent in some private hospitals. Compare World Health Organization guidelines, which say the C-section rate in any region should never be higher than 15 per cent!

Having said that, maternity units in hospitals are certainly not the sterile, clinical places they once were. Great effort has gone into making them more like home. But even though hospital rooms may be attractively decorated and the equipment hidden away in cabinets, the bed is still the central piece of furniture – and chances are that the hospital considers this the appropriate place for you to give birth. If a labour ward is your choice, you can still present a birth plan which should include the freedom to move around, your choice of support people and a vertical rather than horizontal delivery position. With a bit of luck and if all goes well, you'll find that the midwives won't call the doctor until it's really too late for him or her to interfere or to ask you to lie down.

## Birth in water

Whatever you decide, it's worth noting that immersion in water can help you relax through the pain of contractions and shorten the length of the first stage of labour. Birthing pools can be hired and many birth centres (and some hospitals) now incorporate them into their units.

For lots more information on your birthing options and how to develop your own birth plan, see my third book with Francesca Naish, *The Natural Way to Better Birth and Bonding*.

## 3. With whom?

Choose sympathetic birth attendants and ensure they are aware of your plan and your desire for a natural birth.

Once you've made up your mind that you'll give a natural birth your very best shot, and where it's to take place, it's vitally important to choose the right people to support you. In reality, 'where' you give birth is not really the issue – 'with whom' is actually far more important. You need to decide whether you want obstetric or midwifery care and who else – your partner, another relative or friend or even older children – you want to be present. It's important that you feel entirely comfortable with every person who will be there – your carer, partner and other support people.

Women have always been the traditional attendants at births, although in some communities the father actually underwent a mock labour. However, he was rarely present, with female friends and relatives filling most of the roles that today will probably be filled by your husband or life partner.

In the space of a few decades it's become commonplace for a woman's life partner to attend their child's birth. But just make sure that partner really and truly wants to be there. Squeamishness or uncertainty isn't necessarily a sign that person doesn't support you wholeheartedly, but it's a fact that one in ten British men bail out before their baby's born because they find it too stressful. Only 60 per cent of those men are present for the entire labour and birth. That said, after a natural unmedicated labour and birth most partners agree that it was an absolute high point in their life.

Also give some careful thought to the rest of your support team. Studies show that women who receive constant support while giving birth have shorter labours and fewer interventions. So, in addition to your professional carer and/or partner, who else will be there for you? Your mum, a girlfriend who has given birth herself or maybe you'd like to have a doula? Will older children be present? Remember this isn't a circus sideshow or a performance for the curious, this is as intimate as love-making, so choose carefully and once again, be sure that you're completely comfortable with your selection.

## Your professional carer

So is it to be obstetric or midwifery care? Of course the decision you make at the beginning of your pregnancy might change – it might have to change if complications develop – but if there are conflicting views about management, testing, screening or your birth plan, it's absolutely okay to review your choice. You're entitled to get a second opinion or to change your mind – lots of women do. This is your birth!

Although some procedures are still performed routinely in a few unenlightened maternity units, there are many obstetricians who will be happy for your labour to unfold naturally and for you to give birth without intervention. Female obstetricians tend to fall into this category more frequently than males. Also keep in mind that doctors who are registered with birth centres are more likely to be sympathetic to a natural, non-interventionist approach.

Find out which hospitals have the highest (and the lowest) rates of induction, epidurals, episiotomies and C-sections. Be sure to do some homework about induction rates, about what happens if you go beyond your 'due date', about time constraints that may be placed on the first or second stage of labour – that ticking clock not only makes for anxiety but could lead to some sort of procedure 'to get things moving'. After that, it's likely to be the cascade of medical or surgical intervention. For all the details of the intervention that can result, read *The Natural Way to Better Birth and Bonding*.

Hannah Dahlen says that many women and their partners get seduced by the pleasant environment of the hospital, either neglecting or completely oblivious to the statistics that can clearly show the likelihood that their birth will be intervention-free (or otherwise) in their chosen setting. In February 2012, Justine Davies reporting in *Essential Baby/The Sydney Morning Herald*, quoted Dahlen: 'A first-time mother in Australia now has a greater chance of surgical intervention during her birth than of not having it! This is not safe, either physically or psychologically.'

## Obstetric care

If you decide on obstetric care, it's good to have a personal referral from someone who had expectations that were similar to your own and found that their wishes and their birth plan were respected. If you don't have any close friends who've given birth recently, you'll have to do your own research. That may well mean having an initial appointment with two or three doctors. Take your partner or other support person along to the appointments. The obstetrician might be the expert in the white coat, but you're choosing someone who can uphold or hinder your desire for a natural birth and you need to be confident that you're all on the same page.

## Midwifery care

If you choose a midwife, she'll see you for all your antenatal visits. You may go to her home, but in the latter weeks, she'll probably come to yours. If you're opting out of the ultrasounds and diagnostic testing, then she'll honour that choice unless there's a very good reason to perform them. During labour, a midwife will do little more than watch, wait and support. Midwifery training is quite different from that of medical specialists and although a midwife is able to manage emergencies capably and quickly, her role is that of facilitator and caregiver. It is not to intervene, but she can determine if and when intervention is necessary.

Statistics clearly show that there are fewer interventions, and perinatal mortality rates are much lower, when births take place with only a midwife in attendance. An independent midwife is also usually accredited at a birth centre, giving you flexibility with your choice of place of birth. All of that said, midwives have different personalities and even slightly different philosophies and you need to feel absolutely comfortable with your choice.

## Doulas

If you're a little apprehensive about your partner as a support act and you want somebody else in attendance but there's nobody appropriate in your circle of family or friends, your midwife or childbirth educator can put you in touch with a doula. *Doula* is a Greek word that is translated as 'woman's servant'. Though this person is professionally trained to offer guidance, encouragement, advice and any explanations that might be necessary during the birth, she does not actually perform any clinical tasks. But you can be sure that she won't wimp out when things get moving and can be a wonderful support in the postnatal period.

## Your partner's role

So your partner's up for it! He's done the preconception care, together you've made decisions about prenatal testing, about where and with whom your baby will be born and he's got down and dirty at those childbirth education classes. During labour, he'll massage you, rub your back, wipe your brow, apply hot packs and towels and offer encouragement. If you're using a birth pool, he'll be in there with you; if you're on dry land, he'll help you change position and will support you in a squatting position. He can also act as your advocate for non-intervention if that ever becomes an issue and may even be able to catch your baby when he's born and later cut the umbilical cord. Just warn him to be prepared for strong words when his massage is too firm or not firm enough, if the hot packs are too hot or too cold or when he otherwise doesn't measure up to your expectations. Labour is a time when all your inhibitions fly out the window, so warn him well ahead of time that he's not to take any of your harsh words to heart and offer similar words of caution to female partners at the birth.

The bonds that are established after your baby is born are as important for your partner as they are for you. Witnessing the birth of a child is an extraordinarily powerful emotional experience and it sets the scene for continuing involvement and support throughout your child's life. The feeling of intimacy and sharing which you establish together also means your partner won't feel alienated or excluded in those early months, when your baby takes an enormous amount of your love, attention and time.

## Children at the birth

Children from about three years of age, who have been prepared for what to expect, handle the whole experience with amazing equanimity. Introduce them to your pregnancy and birth story through the many excellent books that have clear, simple illustrations and easy-to-understand text. This can be an ongoing process from the earliest days of your pregnancy. Answer their questions honestly and don't force the issue if they're at all reluctant.

Once you're actually in labour don't expect them to be a constant presence. Be prepared for them to miss the whole thing too – but be sure that you've designated their care to a single member of your support team. The last thing you want is to frighten them with unfamiliar noises or with an unusually preoccupied mother.

You can expect less sibling rivalry when your whole family witnesses the birth. Encouraging older children to touch their new brother or sister, to kiss him and hold his hands will enhance their bonding process. Children's anxiety at the arrival of a new baby can be overcome if they don't feel isolated from the birth.

So remember, it's never too soon to start thinking about your birth plan – and talking it through with your support team. It can even become a form of positive affirmation. Be specific – this labour and birth won't be a dress rehearsal.

## 4. The unexpected

You may have a clear birth plan, calm surroundings, nurturing birth attendants – but sometimes things don't go according to plan.

As in all of life, there are no absolute certainties. Despite your careful preparations, your belief in the normality of the birth process and your commitment to avoiding any intervention, the unexpected can happen. Whether or not you need medical management during your labour will depend on the attitudes and beliefs of those involved, as well as on medical criteria.

You may need to make some decisions regarding intervention during your labour, rather than before it. This situation will be made much easier if you've already discussed with your carers what their responses are likely to be in a given situation. You can then include in your birth plan an outline of how you would prefer to deal with likely or possible complications.

I experienced the unexpected first-hand when, seven hours after my perfectly normal, five-hour labour at home, my second son Mikey began to breathe very rapidly and was transferred to an intensive care unit. You can imagine the distress that I felt when my robust 3.5-kilogram baby was hooked up for 36 hours to a battery of tubes and monitors – all the things I had so diligently tried to avoid. That experience made me very aware that when it comes to conception and pregnancy, we're only ever in charge of the ingredients, not the end result.

I composed the following words shortly after that experience.

If you don't get the natural birth you want, find comfort in the fact that there is a greater hand at work. It might sometimes be difficult to accept the wisdom of that hand, but when you do, you can focus on all the positive things that you've done and get on with the very important task of nurturing your baby. If you know that there were ways in which you could have been better prepared, things which could have been managed differently, or perhaps it was simply that omnipotent hand teaching you a little wisdom and humility – accept it, learn from it, let it go and move on.

Mikey recovered fine and the medical experts never determined exactly what his problem was – 'inhaled vernix' was one suggestion. A wise woman coming from a very different place suggested, 'A challenge to everything that you held near and dear!' I wonder . . .

## DID YOU KNOW?

A 2009 media release from the Australian College of Midwives confirms that women cared for by midwives from early pregnancy until well after the birth have fewer admissions to hospital antenatally, less need for epidurals or for any pain relief, fewer episiotomies, more normal births, reduced need for their baby to be admitted to a special care nursery, more success with breastfeeding and less vulnerability to postnatal depression or anxiety.

## 5. Better birth in your hands – good nutrition

We have the evidence – consumption of refined foods reduces the ease of the birthing process. An excellent diet and ongoing supplementation are important factors that support your desire for a natural birth.

Studies carried out in the 1930s by American dentist Dr Weston Price clearly demonstrated that when native communities ate their traditional, unrefined, wholefood diet, they had short labours and easy deliveries. In fact the labours of Inuit women, still eating their traditional diets, were so quick that the Western medical attendants were never able to get there in time to see the birth.

Abundant supplies of vitamins, trace minerals, essential amino and fatty acids and pre- and probiotics are needed to ensure the presence of all the complex and interdependent factors – the hormones, neurotransmitters, prostaglandins and other chemical messengers – that are required to initiate your labour and maintain it efficiently until your baby is born. These same factors are also needed for bonding and breastfeeding to proceed smoothly. Several important reasons to eat well and continue taking your especially designed supplements!

Zinc is particularly important. If your intake of zinc is adequate, you have a good chance of a short labour and less chance of postnatal depression and cracked nipples. Your baby should be content and cry very little, too. Check your zinc status regularly throughout your pregnancy and supplement accordingly. See *Healthy Parents, Healthy Baby* for more details.

## Healthy gut

While having a healthy gut may not directly relate to having a short, straightforward labour, it is so fundamental to your own and your baby's continuing good physical and mental health that it's worth a mention here.

According to practitioners of traditional Chinese medicine (TCM), Western naturopaths and herbalists, digestive health is central to all other elements of health. So it's hardly surprising that increasing numbers of modern researchers point to 'gut dysbiosis' – which is characterised by an overgrowth of pathogens (unhealthy bacteria and other organisms) – together with reduced biodiversity and levels of 'good' gut bacteria, as the cause of a multitude of physical, mental and emotional problems. Compromised gut health can begin at birth, which is why I raise the issue in this chapter, and it can be all downhill from there. Caesarean birth, formula feeding, antibiotics, pesticides in your food, chlorine in your water, refined and genetically modified food, toxins . . . the list of factors that compromise gut health is long and it begins very early in life. To learn more about these factors and for ways to 'restore your gut to health and happiness' and the best products for the job, refer to *Healthy Parents, Healthy Baby*.

But more to the point than the multiple factors contributing to gut dysbiosis are the reasons for establishing a healthy gut population during your pregnancy. Only a brief window of opportunity exists postnatally to establish healthy gut activity in your baby, setting the foundation for a lifetime of better physical and mental health for him. Taking advantage of that window of opportunity is up to you . . .

Babies born vaginally are inoculated with their mother's bacteria on their journey down the birth canal. Left on their skin, these bacteria migrate to the gut and establish a healthy community there. This inoculation with healthy organisms is vital for the baby's immunity, with babies born by caesarean section more likely to suffer from asthma, allergies and infection as they miss out on receiving their mothers' good bacteria during the birth process.

Surprised to hear that those little microorganisms in your gut are so influential? But there's more. Below I've summarised the findings that were tabled by researchers from institutions including Harvard Medical School and Yale University School of Medicine in the United States, Institut Pasteur de Lille in France, Karolinska Institutet in Sweden and Ben-Gurion University in Israel. Gathering in February 2012 in Istanbul, Turkey, for the International Symposium of Probiotics and Prebiotics in Pediatrics, these and other international researchers confirmed the importance of establishing gut health in infancy. Their findings demonstrate that the 1.5 kilograms of (mostly) bacteria that are resident in the human gastrointestinal tract are responsible for a great deal more than digestion of food. Correctly termed 'microbiota', that mass contains 100 times more cells and 100 times more genes than are present in you, which explains why the residents in your gut should be considered as a separate organ, whose healthy function and information-carrying activities establish a foundation for all other health-promoting measures.

Healthy gut microbiota will:

- Establish integrity of the gut lining (reducing the likelihood of allergies)
- Maximise nutrient absorption and vitamin synthesis (optimising and maintaining nutritional status)
- Normalise immune function (80 per cent of immune response is mediated through the gut)
- Optimise energy metabolism (helping to maintain normal weight and prevent obesity)
- Support hormone production and normal hormone balance (of your hypothalamus, pituitary and adrenal glands)
- Normalise neurotransmitter production (reducing the likelihood of anxiety and depression)

So how do you ensure all of these gut-related goodies for your baby?

- A probiotic product during pregnancy, which will establish a healthy gut population. Make sure you and your partner take one. (While the bacterial population of your vagina and gastrointestinal tract is the major influence on that of your baby, the microbial population of your partner will also have some influence due to intimate contact with you.)
- Natural vaginal birth

- Immediate and ongoing breastfeeding
- No antibiotics for you or your baby
- Continuing use of probiotic for both partners during breastfeeding

If you're wondering what to do in the case of a caesarean section, formula feeding or antibiotics, invest in a high-potency probiotic product as soon as you possibly can. Take it yourself if you're breastfeeding your baby; add one that's specific for infants to the bottle of formula if you're not. In fact, the maintenance of good gut health for the whole family should be a priority! That goes for previous children (or other family members) who might have got off to a compromised start in the area of their gastrointestinal health – the research shows that probiotic products can act as a 'surrogate' for Mother Nature.

## DID YOU KNOW?

Archaeologists have found that microorganisms were used as probiotics as long ago as 7000 BC. Cultured milk products appear to have their origins in fresh milk that turned to yoghurt after being carried in an animal skin saddlebag. Many traditional societies consumed a good dose of gut-enhancing microorganisms on a daily basis.

## 6. Better birth in your hands – the right exercise

Labour is aptly named – it's a work-out! But it will be shorter and easier if you've exercised regularly.

What's safe? What's comfortable? What should you avoid? For all the details, make sure that you read the section in *Healthy Parents, Healthy Baby* about exercising in pregnancy. Remember to exercise your pelvic floor as well. You should also incorporate the following special stretching exercises for your active birth – if you want to feel absolutely comfortable in these positions, you'll need to practise them well in advance of going into labour.

## Squatting

Squatting confers lots of benefits. It's the position that Nature designed for giving birth. It will encourage your baby's head to become engaged in the pelvic outlet in the last weeks of your pregnancy and increase the width of your birth canal. Practise a supported squat to begin with, by holding onto a piece of furniture or sitting on a pile of magazines or telephone books.

## Rotating hips

Practise standing with your feet planted firmly on the ground, about shoulder width apart, and experience how good it feels to rotate your hips like a belly dancer. Move them in one direction, then reverse the movement.

## Kneeling

Kneel on a folded towel or blanket with your knees about 30 centimetres apart and your back straight. With your hands on your hips, rotate your pelvis as you did in the standing position. Reverse the direction of the rotation.

## Half kneeling

Bring one knee off the blanket and step forwards with that leg so that it now makes a right angle with the floor. You can rock backwards and forwards and change legs as well. This position is particularly helpful for encouraging dilation of your cervix.

## On all fours

From the kneeling position you can readily move into the all-fours position. Getting down on all fours during labour can help if your baby has assumed a posterior lie or if your contractions become very intense.

Practising all these positions will help you to become familiar with how you're likely to move and what positions might be most comfortable during labour.

## 7. Better birth in your hands – natural remedies

Optimal nutrition, regular exercise and feeling familiar with your support people and surroundings are all important, but there are some physical things and natural remedies that you can also consider in your preparation for a natural birth.

## Well before your due date

Raspberry leaf tea is a favourite among midwives and its positive effects are well documented. It improves and coordinates uterine contractions. Follow directions on the packet for making the tea and drink a cup or two every day during the second and third trimesters.

Herbal remedies have been used traditionally before labour and birth. A medical herbalist will be able to make up an appropriate blend or a good health food shop may have suitable products. The blend might include herbs to calm, tone your uterus, ease pain and speed recovery. Herbal blends are normally taken in advance of the labour, so get your preferred product in good time and follow directions carefully.

By gently stretching and massaging your perineum prior to labour, you can reduce the chance of tearing or of needing an episiotomy. Perineal massage can help accustom you to the burning and stretching sensation of second stage. Use almond or coconut oil and do the massage every day for about six weeks before your due date. Zinc, vitamin E and the essential fatty acids are the important nutrients for tissue and skin integrity. If you've been taking your comprehensive supplements during pregnancy, you'll be getting these nutrients; if not, you can certainly add them to your advantage in the weeks leading up to labour. Choose products that are specific for pregnancy and breastfeeding. You'll find some good options in Jan's Picks at www.flurishh.com.

## At the birth

Have some of your favourite music to play – studies indicate music can help a birthing woman relax and focus on the job at hand. Include soothing pieces that your baby has been exposed to in the womb.

Essential oils can be used to achieve a therapeutic effect in the birth room. Lavender, ylang ylang and sandalwood are just some of the fragrances that can be used to promote calm.

Water can ease the pain of your contractions – take a hot shower or, better still, use a birth pool, which you'll find in many birth units. For a water birth at home, arrange your birth pool in advance and ensure your plumbing arrangements make filling it easy.

Water on the inside is important too – staying well hydrated during your labour means having your support person or midwife remind you to drink. Take a plentiful supply of purified water with you whatever your birth location.

Finally, acupuncture and acupressure, homoeopathy, hypnotherapy, flower essences and reflexology have all been shown to help women achieve an easier birth and a more rapid recovery. The appropriate practitioner can help with treatment in advance of labour or with products to go with you.

## 8. What you'll need

Here's a starting point for your list of must-haves and maybe-haves for the birth and for the days that follow.

I firmly believe that at this time in your life, less is actually more. Preparing your birthing space with candles, sweet-scented oils and soft music – as seductive and beautiful as they are – might seem over the top once your labour gets into full swing, when you're grunting and groaning and focused on nothing more than working with those contractions. By the same token, having too many 'baby things' can detract from the main game. Remember that your baby only needs to be fed and warm and close to you.

With those words in mind, what follows will no doubt look like a very long list of the things you and your baby should have or might like to have during and after the birth. You can add or subtract whatever you feel is appropriate for your situation.

## For you – during labour

- Aromatherapy oils and burner
- Massage oil
- Hot/cold pack
- Small sponge to suck
- Beanbag – although some birth suites provide these
- Lip balm
- Purified water – plenty of it
- Homeopathic, herbal or wildflower remedies for stress and for the birth (see the 'Natural remedies' section in *The Natural Way to Better Birth and Bonding*)
- Wholefood (not sugary) snacks/drinks (for you and your support people)
- Swimsuit for your support person (for the birth pool)
- Hand mirror (to watch your baby make his entry into the world)
- Camera, camcorder or smartphone to record the precious moments of birth

While you're sitting or waiting around for labour to swing into top gear, or when your baby is sleeping peacefully, you might be glad of the following, although when my new baby was sleeping peacefully all I wanted to do was look at him – playing a game of cards never entered my head!

- iPod or MP3 player
- ereader
- Books and/or magazines
- Card games and/or Scrabble

## For you – after the birth
- Nursing nightgowns (or long shirts which button down the front) – at least three
- Tracksuit or dressing-gown – depending on the season, but also because air conditioning in hospitals can get cold
- Warm socks – you can use them as slippers too, suggest two pairs
- Slippers or flip-flops – required in hospitals
- Nursing bras – avoid underwire, choose ones where the whole cup folds away rather than the 'trapdoor' type and make sure they're fitted properly. You may wear them to bed as well in the early days of breastfeeding, so suggest at least four
- Terry-towelling nursing pads – you'll need both the towelling and disposable kinds in the first weeks – suggest 12
- Disposable nursing pads – suggest two boxes
- Sanitary pads – maternity or super absorbency, the stick-on variety is best, suggest three packets
- Snug-fitting briefs – suggest ten
- A comfortable outfit to wear home

## For you – toiletries and other stuff
- Face cloths – suggest two soft ones

- Your normal toiletries kit – forget the make-up for the moment
- Soft tissues and toilet paper – the hospital provisions may not be soft enough
- Ear plugs – you'll need these if you're in a noisy hospital ward
- Mobile phone with your contact list ready – but please don't use it when you're nursing your baby. Better still, let your partner phone, text and email through the birth announcements. Definitely leave your laptop at home
- Pen and diary – you may feel the urge to put pen to paper . . . Guess where my books began?

## For your baby – after the birth

If you're having your baby in hospital, he will probably wear the hospital clothes and use their nappies. Of course you can dress your baby in his own clothes and he'll go home in them. Otherwise, you'll need:

- Disposable nappies (newborn size) – choose the best quality biodegradable ones, suggest several packets
- Nappy liners – suggest two packets
- Terry-towelling nappies – suggest 36
- Nappy fasteners – not those old-fashioned nappy pins
- Nappy covers – the fluffy type, suggest four
- Baby nightgowns which tie at the back – these may be easier for you to manage initially, suggest four
- Jumpsuits – newborns size, although your baby will grow fast, suggest six
- Singlets – with an envelope-type neck, suggest six
- Cardigans – suggest two
- Booties – if it's a winter baby, suggest three
- Hats – ditto, suggest two

- Socks – suggest three pairs
- Cotton blankets for wrapping your baby – at least three
- Pashmina
- Baby sling – get one well in advance and practise tying it. You'll probably take a few days to get comfortable with wearing your baby, but once you've got the knack you'll never look back!

Note: Before you decide between cloth and disposable nappies, read more on the pluses and minuses of each below.

## For your baby – back home

I'm not a big fan of buying brand-new baby accessories – they cost money that you could put away for a rainy day. Having a baby is hardly an isolated event and all the apparatus has a very short shelf life, so try the internet, your local paper or recycled children's clothing stores for second-hand items. Also, friends with older children are happy to pass on used equipment, clothes and toys. (They'll feel very virtuous that all that expensive stuff they bought won't be gathering dust in their garage.)

Just remember – your baby is happiest when he's carried close at all times and when he sleeps with you. So for the moment, forget about the fancy nursery with bassinet, cot and change table, and definitely leave the Rolls-Royce pram on the showroom floor. Apart from baby clothes and nappies, you really need very little extra equipment besides the following:

- Baby sling
- Baby capsule for your car
- Sheepskin
- Small baby bath – some are moulded to give your baby's head support, which makes bathing very easy – although you can

always use the kitchen sink. I've recently seen a very clever upside-down teardrop-shaped design that is completely stable despite sitting on its pointy end, with the baby assuming much the same position he took up in the womb. It's very safe as well, since he can't slip down

- Face cloths
- Soft bath towels – your old ones will be a bit rough on your baby's skin
- Baby wipes – some types can be washed and recycled
- Almond or other organic nut oil for baby massage (coconut is another option – although you may find the smell is not as subtle as the nut oils)
- Witch-hazel or other herbal extracts for use on the umbilical cord
- If you choose disposable nappies – a roll of biodegradable plastic bags in which to dispose of them
- If you choose the cloth nappy option, you'll need:
  - Nappy buckets
  - Robust washing machine
  - Eco-friendly soaking solution and washing powder
  - Clothes line in the sun

# THE BEST OF BIRTH AND BONDING:
# TEST YOUR KNOWLEDGE

Now you've learned all about birth and bonding, you'll find some samples of the *flurishh* learning below. When you've answered the five multiple choice questions that follow, check your scores below. The correct answers to the 250 questions such as these will help you accrue points when you play the *flurishh* game at www.flurishh.com.

1. What's the name of the hormone that relaxes muscles and ligaments as pregnancy progresses and helps your pelvis to open?
1. Oxytocin
2. Oestrogen
3. Relaxin
4. Prolactin

2. Which statement most closely reflects your understanding of active birth and your preparation for it?
1. I expect I'll have my legs up in stirrups
2. I will squat in the second stage to open the birth canal fully and reduce tearing
3. If I lie down, my baby will be pushing against gravity
4. My obstetrician says I don't need any preparation

3. Zinc is a vitally important trace element for every stage of reproduction. Making sure your zinc levels are optimal can help to ensure . . .
1. No stretch marks
2. Strong uterine contractions and robust perineal tissue

3. No cracked nipples or postnatal depression
4. All of the above

4. Your gut can be considered as a second brain, producing hormones, neurotransmitters and other chemical messengers. A healthy gut is populated with . . .
1. Pathogens
2. Friendly bacteria
3. Multiple strains of good bacteria that are specific to the human intestines
4. Multiple strains of good bacteria which are passed to the baby during a vaginal birth and breastfeeding

5. You're hoping to have a natural birth. What do you consider the most important feature when checking out a likely location?
1. Positive response from other parents
2. Welcoming rooms, looks like home, monitoring equipment out of sight
3. Allows partners and older children to be present
4. Their low rates of induction and caesarean sections, especially for first-time mums

Answers
**Q1:** 1. 0 pts, 2. 0 pts, 3. 4 pts, 4. 0 pts; **Q2:** 1. 0 pts, 2. 4 pts, 3. 2 pts, 4. 0 pts; **Q3:** 1. 1 pt, 2. 3 pts, 3. 3 pts, 4. 4 pts; **Q4:** 1. 0 pts, 2. 2 pts, 3. 3 pts, 4. 4 pts; **Q5:** 1. 1 pt, 2. 2 pts, 3. 2 pts, 4. 4 pts

(The maximum possible score is 20.)

# CHAPTER 2

## Breastfeeding success

### 1. Breastfeeding – it's best for everybody!

Breastfeeding is the easiest and healthiest way to nourish and nurture your child; in fact, it's good for the whole family.

### 2. Formula – who uses it?

Breastmilk is a dream product, yet use of formula is on the rise around the world.

### 3. Trust your instinct

In an age of information overload, instinct often gets pushed aside. But as a new mum, you have to learn to trust it.

### 4. Breastfeeding – more than nutrition

Breastfeeding is best – there's no question about it! It offers a multitude of benefits that extend way beyond what's good for your baby.

### 5. Nature's tranquillisers and love drugs

Feeling good, calm, connection, bonding, intimacy, trust . . . all delivered by the hormones oxytocin and prolactin.

## 6. The family bed

Recent brain scans confirm the negative effects on infants sleeping separately from their mums.

## 7. Whatever happened to sex?

Wondering where she went – that highly libidinous woman you were before you conceived and while you were pregnant . . . ? Well, she'll be back!

# 1. Breastfeeding – it's best for everybody!

Breastfeeding is the easiest and healthiest way to nourish and nurture your child; in fact, it's good for the whole family.

As a firm advocate for ad hoc and prolonged breastfeeding, whenever I see a bottle-feeding mum I can't help but wonder what influenced her decision. When overwhelming evidence establishes breastmilk as the superior form of nutrition for infants (and toddlers), yet breastfeeding rates stay static or actually decline, it's clear that there is no simple answer to the question. There are often complicated issues at play when a mum decides to put her baby on a bottle – a decision that leaves many women feeling guilty or defensive.

However, my intention in making very obvious my passion for breastfeeding is not to make you uncomfortable. Rather, if I can clarify the important foundation measures that support the early establishment of breastfeeding which results in a greater likelihood that it will continue, if I can outline the simplicity and ease of breastfeeding and the multiple health benefits of breastmilk that extend far beyond healthy food and drink, I hope that you might choose prolonged rather than short-term breastfeeding, that you might delay your decision to introduce formula, or at least not make breast versus bottle an either/or choice.

So let's start with a quote that actually appeared in my earlier book *The Natural Way to Better Breastfeeding*, which is attributed to UNICEF ('Take the Baby-Friendly Initiative!', 1991).

Imagine that the world had invented a new 'dream product' to feed and immunise everyone born on earth. Imagine also that it was available everywhere, required no storage or delivery, helped mothers to plan their families and reduced their risk of cancer. Then imagine that the world refused to use it! At the end of a century of unprecedented discovery and invention, even as scientists discover the origin of life itself, this scenario is alas not a fiction. The dream product is human breast milk.

In other words, you've got it constantly on tap, it's an unlimited supply, always at the right temperature, bound to please even the fussiest customer, with benefits that far outstrip any of its competitors, and it's free! If you had a money-bearing tree in your backyard, that knew no seasons and whose crop was constantly replenished, would you go to the bank, struggle to get a loan approved, be subject to the vagaries of usurious interest rates and lock yourself into debt for the rest of your life, leaving the unpicked money at home on your tree?

The fact that numerous Western women have no exposure to or experience of breastfeeding as a simple, natural, uncomplicated activity is undoubtedly to blame for a great many 'failures' and for their choice to bottle-feed. However, in the context of breastfeeding, negative words such as 'failure', 'breast refusal' and 'poor supply' are studiously avoided by Dr Christina Smillie, an American paediatrician whose clinic is dedicated solely to working with nursing mums and babies. Smillie links the use of these highly emotive words, especially when a new mother's emotional state makes her so susceptible to suggestion, to many of the negative experiences that make a woman turn to formula or cause her professional carer to recommend it. In Smillie's clinical practice, women receive only encouragement and support and lots of time to get things right, based on her firm belief that breastfeeding is actually intuitive for both the infant and the mother and that the 'problems' so many encounter are a relatively recent phenomenon. Smillie cites only references in the historical literature to 'the baby taking the breast' and 'the mother giving the breast'.

This simplicity and ease is certainly observed in many countries that still consider breastfeeding to be the primary form of feeding infants and young children. *007 Breasts*, reporting on how breast-feeding is seen around the world, tells us that in Ghana, where bottle-feeding is for orphans, 'if a baby cries and you do not breast feed, people draw the conclusion the baby is not yours'. In the majority of African countries it is normal to see a mother breast-feeding in public, with a non-breastfeeding mum frowned upon in some communities. Years rather than months is the normal breast-feeding period and even in cultures that are otherwise very modest, breastfeeding a baby in public is considered absolutely normal, with special shirts or draped materials obscuring the breast from view. These enduring attitudes in the developing world, while under threat thanks to the inroads of Western influence, ensure that the average breastfeeding period worldwide is still a little over four years.

If that statistic surprises you, another one for reflection is found in Kathy Dettwyler's anthropological research on what constitutes the normal length of lactation. She wrote that all primates lactate for six times their period of gestation. Doing the sum ($6 \times 9 = 54$ months), she calculated that the appropriate breastfeeding period for human beings would be considered as 4.5 years!

While the former statistics may not be widely known, the following pronouncements from influential institutions are readily available, widely disseminated and unanimous in their recommendation to breastfeed and for a prolonged period at that. The American Academy of Pediatrics, American Academy of Family Physicians, Australian Breastfeeding Association, International Lactation Consultant Association, World Health Organization and many more all say the same thing:

- Breastmilk exclusively for the first six months. (I say: nothing extra, no solids or complementary formula prior to this.)
- Breastfeed for as long as mutually desired. (I say: let your baby decide when he's had enough.)

- Breastfeed for up to two years and beyond. (I say: the belief that breastmilk is only for babies needs to go.)
- There is no upper limit to the duration of breastfeeding nor evidence of psychological or developmental harm from breastfeeding into the third year of life or longer. (I say: just keep breastfeeding.)

I would add here that if formula does become your choice at any stage, there is great value in continuing some level of breastfeeding – and here are the reasons why:

- Breastmilk is species specific – that means human milk for human babies (and cow's milk for calves, etc.).
- The composition of breastmilk is perfectly suited to your baby's stage of development (and differs for a premmie baby).
- The composition of breastmilk changes during a feed but also during the day.
- Breastmilk contains a wide range of health-promoting compounds, the composition of which differs from those found in the milk of other species. These compounds include carbohydrates, nucleotides, fatty acids, immunoglobulins, cytokines, immune cells, lysozyme, lactoferrin and other immune-modulating factors.
- The multiple immune-stimulating factors in breastmilk mean fewer allergies, reduced incidence of atopic conditions, fewer infections and reduced likelihood of auto-immune conditions such as type 1 diabetes.
- Breastmilk contains prebiotic substances – human milk oligosaccharides (HMOS). These are the third largest component after lactose and lipids and are extremely complex, consisting of at least 1000 different compounds. They cannot be duplicated in any formula.

- Colostrum (the bright yellow 'first milk' that is produced in the days following the birth) is particularly high in HMOS.
- HMOS ensure the growth of specific, healthy intestinal bacteria and inhibit the adhesion of infectious bacterial pathogens or bacterial toxins to the gut wall.
- Breastmilk also contains the bacteria that set up a lifetime of better gut health for the infant. I might sound like a record stuck in a groove, but lack of these health-promoting bacteria in infancy is linked to the development of some of the most pressing physical and mental health issues of our time, such as obesity and depression.
- Lactoferrin, another substance promoting intestinal health, and lysozyme, an antimicrobial, are both high in breastmilk.
- Breastmilk contains living white blood cells and immuno-globulins – further immune-enhancing factors.
- Breastmilk is rich in the omega-3 essential fatty acids. Their chemical names shortened to DHA and AA, these substances are vital for the formation and development of your baby's brain and eyes.
- Breastmilk contains the fat-digesting enzyme lipase, which accounts for the bland-smelling nappies of the breastfed baby. Lipase is absent in formula.
- The protein component of breastmilk is easily digested and more completely absorbed than protein in formula.
- Sleep-inducing proteins are high in breastmilk and the concentration of tryptophan (needed by the body to make melatonin, which also promotes sleep) is higher in night-time breastmilk.
- Vitamins and minerals in breastmilk are easily absorbed. In contrast to 50–75 per cent absorption of iron from breastmilk, only 5–10 per cent of iron is absorbed from formula.

- Breastmilk contains hormones such as prolactin and oxytocin. Read more on the important roles of these hormones in 'Nature's tranquillisers and love drugs' to follow.
- The mother's diet affects the taste of her breastmilk and is therefore influential in accustoming her child to the cultural diet. Formula always tastes exactly the same.

The list goes on and each year the evidence mounts, as more and more factors are identified and their role in establishing and maintaining health in infancy and throughout adult life are elucidated. It will probably come as no surprise that the benefits extend to the breast-feeding mum as well and I'll talk more about those in the following sections.

## DID YOU KNOW?

Drawing on data from 10,000 children, Dr Maria Iacovou from the Institute for Social and Economic Research at Essex University, UK showed that feeding on demand is associated with higher IQ scores at the age of eight, and better performance in national curriculum tests at ages five, seven, eleven and fourteen.

## 2. Formula – who uses it?

Breastmilk is a dream product, yet use of formula is on the rise around the world.

Before I come to all the factors that can help ensure successful and long-term breastfeeding, perhaps a brief review of the status quo might be appropriate. Despite breastfeeding being the established method of feeding for most Western mums on discharge from hospital, the rate declines sharply month by month and by the end of 12 months, more than 80 per cent of Western women have weaned their baby and turned to formula. Ironically, the nearer a modern mum is to modern hospitals, the greater the likelihood that she will stop breastfeeding! What's more, in the United States only 32 per cent of women breastfeed exclusively for four months and a tiny 12 per cent breastfeed exclusively for six months, with the rate of breastfeeding among black women significantly lower than for whites.

These statistics don't reflect well on either professionals or parents, given levels of education and support and those recommendations from World Health Organization and others. In fact, if breastfeeding were practised in the first hour of life, according to a 2006 study published in the journal *Pediatrics*, it could save 41 per cent of newborns who would otherwise die in their first month of life, with other estimates suggesting that 1.5 million children worldwide die every year as a direct result of not being breastfed.

Despite all the positive publicity, the encouraging recommendations and the ban against advertising infant formula, breastfeeding rates are sadly in decline in developing countries. In their helter-skelter embrace of all things Western – which are the symbols in those nations of increasing success and affluence – artificial formula has become in the minds of many, the very best way to ensure a healthy baby. 'If Western women do it, we should do it too' seems to be their attitude.

Finally and further compounding the move to artificial feeding, and certainly perpetuating the belief that breastfeeding is not something as normal and natural as your circulation or your digestion, are tacit confirmations of the difficulty and of the need for a substitute, which can be found on every single can of infant formula: 'For those women who cannot or do not want to breastfeed . . .'

But there's a glimmer of light at the end of the tunnel! In February 2012, the media reported that singer and first-time mum Beyoncé had fed her seven-week-old baby in public, and at a table of a prestigious restaurant in New York's West Village no less. While you may not get excited by this bit of breastfeeding gossip, other celebrities have now weighed in to the debate. Actress Jenna Elfman, a spokeswoman for the breastfeeding advocacy group Best for Babes, describes Beyoncé feeding Blue Ivy at the table as a 'classy example that breast-feeding is and should be a natural part of our life as a society'. Dr Alison Stuebe, an Assistant Professor for the Division of Maternal Fetal Medicine at the University of North Carolina, offered further support, as reported by American news source ABC News ('Breastfeeding Advocates Praise Beyoncé for Nursing Daughter in Public', 1 March 2012): 'By bringing breastfeeding into the mainstream, Beyoncé can help break down barriers so that mothers and babies can breastfeed in peace.'

Beyoncé's shining example occurs at the same time that instances of NIP (a beautifully appropriate acronym that actually stands for Nursing in Public) are making headlines. Many US nursing mothers, it seems, are fed up with retreating to public bathrooms or other out-of-public-view places to feed their babies and are staging nurse-ins to assert their right to breastfeed wherever and whenever.

I remain eternally optimistic that there is a groundswell of committed families (because this commitment must include dads too) that know what is best for their baby. Your own confidence in and commitment to breastfeeding is a wonderful way to spread the message, so now let's look at the factors that are likely to ensure your own breastfeeding success and in ensuring that, arm you with the information to silence any critics or doubters and allow you to support other families in their breastfeeding journey.

## 3. Trust your instinct

In an age of information overload, instinct often gets pushed aside. But as a new mum, you have to learn to trust it. When it comes to breastfeeding, your own positive attitude can be helped by applying a very healthy dose of maternal instinct. And luckily Mother Nature is on your side, with the breastfeeding hormone oxytocin actually encouraging your right-brained instinctive response. That's all very well, but if you're not breastfeeding yet, how can you get in touch with that intuitive, instinctive side of your brain?

At some time in your life, and certainly at some time during your years as a parent, you'll know without any doubt that you made an unwise decision. You'll know because you paid no heed to an insistent inner voice – your instinct. Instinct is a powerful urge that guides you constantly, yet for the most part you're unaware of it until you ignore it. But when you do, you'll get a distinctly uncomfortable feeling, a churning in your insides that prompts you to think again or a very strong sense of going against what your heart dictates.

Unfortunately, in this day and age, when so many decisions are left-brain, logical, rational ones, the purely right-brain, instinctive ones get pushed aside. New research around our 'enteric' brain also tells us that there is very real intelligence that is commonly referred to as 'gut' feeling, while there's also a third brain centred in our heart. Each one is responsible for a different type of decision and when all three are aligned you can be sure you're making the right one. This research provides evidence that statements such as 'I had a feeling in my gut that it was wrong' or 'My heart just ached to listen to her crying' are not just throwaway lines but come from a deep-seated and intuitive understanding of intelligences that are older and wiser than the logical, rational reasoning that goes on in your head.

This is a simplistic summation of a new and very exciting topic – more on our three brains at another time and place. But for now, suffice to say that instinct and intuitive responses really kick in big-time when you become a mum or a dad and those responses are very wise, so don't ignore them!

# Getting in touch with your instinct

Listen politely to all the advice, because you'll get plenty. Your own mother, your mother-in-law, your sister, your girlfriends, the clinic nurse, other health professionals, even perfect strangers will all have something to offer. Train yourself to notice how you feel as each piece of potential wisdom is dispensed.

- 'How does my gut feel?'
- 'Does this make my heart sing?'
- 'What do I really think about this?'

This is a great way to start sifting through the useless advice and to get in touch with what actually resonates with you. Because, after all, this is about you and your baby!

Every mum and dad is different, and every baby is different. So if you hear that nursing your newborn whenever he cries is 'making a rod for your own back', don't let your baby cry simply because that advice came from Grandma who raised six kids and should know. Crying babies stir extraordinary emotions in both women and men (current mothers and fathers and those long past the stage) – they're designed that way. Pick up your crying baby – it's what he needs.

Do the litmus test with everything that you hear. Ask yourself, How would I feel if I did that?, or, What do I really believe is right? Sometimes it's useful to ask yourself, What would a woman in a traditional society do? While you can't go back to tribal ways, you might just learn something from observing older practices.

Trust that feeling in your gut, listen to what your heart is telling you, leave the analytical, rational brain for now or at least only bring it to bear after you've asked the support cast (i.e., the other brains) for their response. The more you go with your gut feeling and your heart attachments, the better you get at your parenting role.

## Stay close to your baby

There was a time when the only thing that you needed for your newborn was some fabric to bind him close to your body. Now almost everything you're invited to acquire is designed to keep you and your baby separate. A nursery, a pram, stroller, bassinet, cot, swing, bouncinette, playpen and, more recently, electronic monitors and sensors (more on those in Chapter 6: Be clean and green), to list just some of the items that will reduce your ability to respond instinctively to your baby and to accurately intuit his needs. When your baby's an extension of you, the difference in how you respond will be dramatic. If you don't think your response would ever match up to those African mums who know when their naked baby is about to empty his bowels, try carrying him close and see how much more attuned to his needs you become and how much more instinctively you respond.

Both your breastfeeding relationship and those instinctive responses are also honed when your whole family sleeps together. Read more below, in 'The family bed', for the long-term benefits. They might surprise you.

## Nutritional factors

Believe it or not, nutritional factors have an influence on maternal and paternal instinct. You need plenty of the trace elements zinc and manganese – animal studies show that low levels of both minerals cause a mother to neglect her young. Trusting your maternal instinct can be hard too if your baby is less than optimally healthy. Everything I've talked about is designed to avoid that eventuality, but it's important that you continue with all of your healthy choices – don't let them slip just because your baby is in your arms. To make sure your baby's getting plenty of premium-grade breastmilk, take your supplements every day.

Women in many traditional societies ate the placenta to restore the status of zinc and other trace elements in the days and weeks following the birth. Of course that tradition may not sit very comfortably with women today, but happily modern technology can come to your aid with placenta-encapsulation services – that is, having the placenta turned into pill form. Consumption of the placenta has genuine therapeutic effects. Actress January Jones attested to these after she gave birth to a son in September 2011. She told People.com: 'Your placenta gets dehydrated and made into vitamins. It's something I was very hesitant about, but we're the only mammals who don't ingest our own placentas. It's not witchcrafty or anything! I suggest it to all mums!'

## 4. Breastfeeding – more than nutrition

Breastfeeding is best – there's no question about it! It offers a multitude of benefits that extend way beyond what's good for your baby.

Despite many new developments and innovations in artificial formulas, none of these products can hope to imitate Nature. Not only is breast best for your baby, it's best for you, for the whole family, for the community and for the planet.

Breastmilk is an extraordinarily complex substance, and the interactions and psychological development that accompany the act of breastfeeding are equally complex. Quite simply, it is presumptuous of humankind to think that we could manufacture a substance that could duplicate breastmilk and that a bottle could replace the interplay and exchange that occurs when a baby nurses at his mother's breast.

### Benefits of breastfeeding – for your baby

Let's look at the benefits to your baby. For starters, breastmilk soothes and settles an unhappy child at any time of the day or night. Breastfed kids cope better with stress than their formula-fed peers, and the calming effects seem to last for years after they have been weaned. It's also the only way to ensure the optimal development of your baby's brain, eyes, digestive and immune systems. Breastfeeding protects your child against a range of illnesses and infections, such as middle ear, gastrointestinal, respiratory and urinary tract infections. Breastfed babies are also less likely to suffer from asthma or eczema or from more serious conditions, such as childhood diabetes or leukaemia.

## Benefits of breastfeeding – for you

Breastmilk is convenient – it's always available and requires no preparation or special storage, a benefit that really can't be over-emphasised. And breastfeeding is good for you too – under the influence of oxytocin, your uterus returns quickly to its normal size and shape after the birth, and it confers lactational amenorrhoea (that means no periods for a while – more on this below).

Breastfeeding mothers are also well bonded to their infants and much less likely to abuse or harm their children and, into the future, are protected from breast and ovarian cancer, suffer fewer symptoms at menopause, have reduced risk of post-menopausal heart attack and stroke and less chance of fractures from osteoporosis. And the longer the period of breastfeeding, the greater the benefits!

## Promoting successful long-term breastfeeding

- ✓ Start sun baths during pregnancy. A modest amount of sun on your nipples is great preparation for delicate tissue that's going to get a work-out.
- ✓ Make sure your zinc status is adequate. This will ensure robust connective tissue, reducing the risk of cracked nipples.
- ✓ Place your baby on your chest immediately after birth – skin on skin.
- ✓ Nurse your baby as soon as he's ready. Weighing and measuring can wait.

✓ Make sure your baby is in the right position. You should feel comfortable, and there should be no pain.

✓ Until you get used to nursing, it's easier if you can always be skin on skin.

✓ Say no to swaddling, which stabilises the baby but nothing else. It interferes with all positive mother–baby interactions.

✓ Let your baby initiate his feeding. American paediatrician Christina Smillie tells women that instincts start the feeding process then successful transfer of milk teaches your baby and he gradually moves from instinctive to learned process.

✓ Feeding must always be a mutually comfortable relationship.

✓ One feed, one breast – the engorgement will probably indicate which one is due next, otherwise attach something on the appropriate side to remind you.

✓ Get a well-designed nursing bra – avoid the trapdoor type, which limits skin-on-skin contact, and make sure it is fitted correctly.

✓ Your baby will have small frequent feeds in his early days, so throw the clock away!

✓ Avoid the use of pacifiers.

✓ Supply equals demand – the more your baby feeds, the more milk your breasts produce. Complementary formula feeds, used as a top-up, are totally counterproductive.

✓ Wear your baby.

✓ Sleep beside him – despite earnestly held beliefs, babies were not designed to sleep alone.

✓ Babies were not designed to sleep through the night, either – the fact some do is not a measure of 'good baby' behaviour!

✓ Remember that your baby only needs food, drink and comfort – and all of those he gets at your breast.

✓ When your baby sleeps during the day, do the same – forget the housework and the shopping and get any of your other kids to lie down with you too. Any rest period is important in maintaining milk supply which is often low late in the day.

✓ Make sure your partner understands all the benefits of breastfeeding (and of prolonged breastfeeding). You may have to educate him to get his full support.

✓ A plentiful supply of breastmilk and your best chance of long-term breastfeeding depends on a really healthy diet and lots of high-quality purified water. Remember to keep taking your supplements too.

✓ Keep stress levels to a minimum – you'll find lots of recommendations in *Healthy Parents, Healthy Baby*.

✓ Your fully breastfed baby may be smaller than other babies of the same age, but not necessarily lighter – he'll have denser bones and more muscle. Don't pay too much attention to the graphs and charts of the paediatricians and clinic sisters – many of them are based on a bottle-fed population.

✓ Ask the experts about weaning – only three-year-olds need apply!

## DID YOU KNOW?

Breastfeeding right after the birth increases the likelihood that your baby will continue to breastfeed. That's another reason to avoid a medicated labour and birth!

## 5. Nature's tranquillisers and love drugs

Feeling good, calm, connection, bonding, intimacy, trust . . . all delivered by the hormones oxytocin and prolactin.

When you breastfeed, raised levels of prolactin are produced by your pituitary gland. Prolactin is the hormone that controls lactation and it also has a calming, sedative effect on both you and your baby.

Another result of increased prolactin production is that ovulation is delayed. In the absence of an ovulation cycle, normal ovarian hormones such as oestrogen won't peak once a month to trigger the release of an egg, delaying the return of your period and meaning the unlikelihood of another pregnancy while you're breastfeeding. Caution is required here, however – watch for signs and symptoms of returning fertility which will predate your period.

At the same time, oxytocin, secreted into the bloodstream, is also produced by the nerve endings, where it acts as a signalling substance. Its action on smooth muscle is responsible for uterine contractions during labour and the let-down reflex during breast-feeding. Oxytocin is also the hormone promoting calm, connection, love, intimacy and stress reduction – the counter to the fight-or-flight response – and breastfeeding women and their babies get an unlimited supply of it.

The oxytocin research team at Karolinska Institutet in Sweden say that animals who receive as litle as one dose per day for five days need little additional oxytocin to stay calm for up to three weeks. Dr Kerstin Uvnäs-Moberg, who heads the team and has published more than 400 papers, stresses oxytocin's ability to grow or develop people's relaxation and restoration capacity. Uvnäs-Moberg's research has identified a wide variety of positive physiological and behavioural responses that are due to oxytocin. They include gastro-intestinal and cardiovascular effects with affirmation and affection decreasing levels of the stress hormone cortisol.

Oxytocin produced by a breastfeeding mother means that she seeks more time with her infant, will initiate further breastfeed-ing, exhibits a greater degree of stroking and calming behaviour and, significantly, has a much greater tolerance for monotony! But to my mind, the most important fact is that oxytocin inhibits left-brain function! Oxytocin ensures a complete left-brain deficit after childbirth – that means that your right brain is the dominant force, which enhances your intuitive responses. This very important factor enables you to lose track of time and to be blissfully unaware of when your baby last fed or slept. That wonderful, foggy 'baby brain' that so many women deride is a completely understandable and healthy adaptation to this new phase of life. Trying to get back to your old busy, well-ordered, tightly scheduled life, or watching the clock and keeping a feeding or sleeping log of your new baby, when you should be enjoying this period of calm, connection and, yes, monotony, is completely counterproductive and the antithesis of what Nature designed for you both. When you allow your intuitive interaction to rule, you co-regulate your baby's nervous system, help him adapt to rapid changes, cope with stress and lay down brain pathways.

Breastfeeding truly is one powerful activity and oxytocin is one powerful hormone! Just remember, the benefits of oxytocin and prolactin – calm and patience, reduced stress levels, enhanced bonding and nurturing and other positive effects that last a lifetime – do not come in a bottle. They come when you breastfeed!

## 6. The family bed

Recent brain scans confirm the negative effects on infants sleeping separately from their mums.

Trust me – co-sleeping, which simply means having your baby within arm's reach, isn't a trendy parenting alternative nor is it designed to promote unhealthily dependent children. It's simply a night-time arrangement that humankind has enjoyed for most of our time on the planet – and it's easy. It's also what Nature designed to foster optimally secure and healthy babies and minimally disturbed nursing mums (and sleeping dads).

I will always remember with gratitude a girlfriend who had recently given birth (at home), extolling the virtues of taking her baby into the family bed after the birth and letting him stay. When I heard her story, it just felt so right. Remember, that warm feeling of 'rightness' in your guts is equally as telling as the cold, churning one that says 'wrong'. Pregnant at the time with my first son, I knew immediately that's what I would do – I also assumed I'd get flak, thought there'd be snide comments, the usual naysaying. But do you know what surprised me? Once Dave was born and I shared details of our family sleeping arrangements with friends and acquaintances, lots of mums and dads confessed to sleeping with their babies. Admittedly for many it was done as a last resort when multiple wakings, trips from a comfy bed to the nursery and feedings repeated ad nauseam resulted in sleep deprivation and total exhaustion. The resolve of those parents to maintain separate sleeping quarters took varying periods of time to crumble, so my question is, why wait until you're sleep deprived and exhausted? Why wait until your baby's normal sleep–wake cycle has been disturbed by sleeping alone? There's no doubt in my mind that my boys' security and confidence was fostered in part by our sleeping arrangements and that my strong instinctive response to those arrangements was right.

## Benefits of co-sleeping – for your baby and you

Your newborn baby is a very light sleeper – that means he'll wake frequently. Light sleep and easy arousal are unique features of his early months, but they're features that are vitally important for his brain development. He wasn't designed to sleep for unbroken hours at a stretch!

When you sleep with your baby, your sleep and arousal patterns synchronise with his. Your arousal–sleep–arousal cycle lasts about 90 minutes, which is also the usual length of time between feeds for your co-sleeping baby. This mightn't seem like a lot of time between feeds, but it's exactly what your baby's developing brain needs.

The wonderful thing about co-sleeping is that you'll be in the arousal part of your cycle just as your baby wakes and begins to nurse. If he's right beside you, he may not even cry; instead, he'll just latch on and you'll probably fall asleep again as he suckles. As he gets older, and both of you become accustomed partners in this night-time dance, you'll hardly even notice. Even though you and your co-sleeping baby are aroused more often, your total sleep time is numerically greater. What's more, the studies show that co-sleeping mothers only remember half of their baby's wakings and feedings and 94 per cent say they have had 'enough' sleep. Reckon those separate-sleeping mums can say the same?

Babies that co-sleep cry less and for shorter periods and gain weight faster. Importantly, the co-sleeping baby maintains easy arousal even when sleeping alone, protecting him from Sudden Infant Death Syndrome, or SIDS. By contrast, the average sleep cycle of the solitary baby is about 200 minutes, and he spends a much greater length of time in deep sleep from which he is not easily aroused. A co-sleeping baby also responds to his mother's (or his father's) breathing and his apnoea rate is reduced. The mechanisms regulating your baby's respiratory rate, heart rate, oxygen saturation level and other significant factors operate better when your baby is in direct contact with you or your partner.

## What the experts say

James McKenna, Professor of Biological Anthropology and Director of the Mother–Baby Behavioral Sleep Laboratory, at the University of Notre Dame, USA, and author of multiple publications such as 'Why Babies Should Never Sleep Alone: A review of the co-sleeping controversy in relation to SIDS, bed sharing and breast feeding', has this to say: 'Solitary sleeping arrangements represent one of the least recognised, but certainly one of the most potentially significant cultural experiments of the 19th and 20th centuries, the consequences of which have never been scientifically explored.' Also in that publication, McKenna states: 'Human infant milk composition necessitates short intervals between breast feeds making human mother–infant co-sleeping not only expectable but biologically necessary.' He argues that the nursing mother–baby dyad is actually biologically designed to sleep as a unit. 'Breastfeeding and co-sleeping are part of the same adaptive system that maximizes infant survival and parental reproductive success.'

Margot Sunderland, Director of Education at the Centre for Child Mental Health in London and one of Britain's leading experts in children's mental health, also advises parents to adopt co-sleeping until their child is at least five. Sunderland affirms that the practice of co-sleeping makes children more likely to grow up as calm and healthy adults. Sunderland's recommendations are based on the most current research on brain development and scans that are now able to demonstrate clearly how babies and children respond to separation. Aware of the difficulties of overturning years of convention and of overriding some strongly held prejudices against children in the parental bed, Sunderland put it very bluntly in a *Sunday Times* interview ('Children "Should Sleep with Parents until They're Five"', Sian Griffiths, 14 May 2006): 'There is absolutely no study saying it is good to let your child cry.'

My money is firmly on McKenna's and Sunderland's recommendations. Sunderland has gone on to say that moving children to their own bed from a few weeks old, despite the fact that they cry through the night, increases their production of cortisol. Remember that elevated levels of cortisol, one of the hormones that the body produces under stress, have been linked to health issues such as high blood pressure, constriction of blood vessels, headaches, gut problems, reduced attachment and compromised bonding, breast-feeding difficulties, failure to thrive and develop, reduced IQ and social distrust.

Of course the old recommendations that you must accustom your baby to sleeping alone and to self-settling from very early days are still doing the rounds and I expect they will for a good while yet. Likewise, some dubious studies that suggest co-sleeping infants are at risk have made no allowance for extenuating circumstances, such as the presence of inappropriate beds and bedding materials and of smoking, drinking and drug-taking parents.

Now you know the benefits of co-sleeping, get yourself organised with the best arrangement for you – a king-size mattress on the floor was my choice, but there are sidecar arrangements that work well too. But the operative word is easy!

And before I say goodnight, a little bit of fun that I wrote for a young friend's baby shower. She had suggested to all the party-goers that a small contribution to a new cot for her unborn would be appreciated.

You say a cot . . .
but maybe not?
The family bed
is good instead!
For night-time feeds
and night-time needs.
Stay horizontal, warm and snug –
the nursery option is a dud!
Mum least disturbed,
Bub least distressed.
Don't leave your bed –
just bare the breast.
A sidecar so she will not fall
or mattresses placed wall to wall.
It's easy, best . . . what more to say?
Ignore the doubters who say nay!

The world has always slept this way . . .

and she WILL leave your bed one day!

AND long before she goes to university – that's a promise!

Happy co-sleeping!

## DID YOU KNOW?

A recent neurological study showed that a child separated from a parent experienced similar brain activity to one in physical pain.

## 7. Whatever happened to sex?

Wondering where she went – that highly libidinous woman you were before you conceived and while you were pregnant . . . ? Well, she'll be back!

If you've just had a baby, you may be wondering, whatever happened to sex? There's a good chance that if you're not, your partner is! The lustful, libidinous you of your 'trying to conceive' and pregnant days is a distant memory. Just relax – rest assured that you're quite normal and Nature actually conspires against you, especially when you're breastfeeding. Nature has a vested interest in making sure your newborn gets the best of your time and energy stores without the competition from another pregnancy or another sibling.

Different cultures have strictures that are designed to achieve the same thing – that it's considered bad form for children to be born very close together. In Sierra Leone, for instance, post-birth sexual abstinence lasts for a full year, while in some Pacific Island cultures it lasts for two. Some cultures condone the father taking a mistress while his wife is breastfeeding their child – unlikely to be a popular solution in our culture that values (at least in theory) the practice of monogamy. But it's worth knowing there are good precedents for your lack of libido. There are physiological ones too.

During breastfeeding, your pituitary gland produces raised levels of prolactin, which means no ovulation, the time in your cycle when your libido is actually at its peak – so that's one reason why sex may be far from your thoughts.

There's another factor at play here too. Oxytocin, the hormone responsible for the let-down reflex, is the same hormone that is released at orgasm. So when you're breastfeeding you might be getting the equivalent of a dozen or more orgasms every day! Oxytocin is also produced thanks to the constant skin-to-skin contact you're having with your baby. Remember I said that you'd both be awash in a sea of oxytocin – I wasn't kidding!

Being aware of the reasons for your lack of sexual interest, you can work on ways to circumvent Nature's handiwork. Penetrative sex is not the only way to express your love for your partner. The important thing is that you take your return to sexual activity at a pace that feels right for you and that your partner understands that your lack of interest isn't a personal thing. Talk about it, laugh about it; just don't let it lead to resentment.

Keep in mind also that when your sex life does return to something approaching normal, the lack of periods that you may be enjoying due to breastfeeding is not a totally foolproof contraceptive. You'll find sound advice for appropriate contraception at this time in my fourth book with Francesca Naish, *The Natural Way to Better Breastfeeding*.

# BREASTFEEDING SUCCESS:
# TEST YOUR KNOWLEDGE

Now you've learned all about how to establish and promote successful long-term breastfeeding, you'll find some samples of the *flurishh* learning below. When you've answered the five multiple choice questions that follow, check your scores below. The correct answers to the 250 questions such as these will help you accrue points when you play the *flurishh* game at www.flurishh.com.

1. Inaccurate information makes it hard for new, breastfeeding mums. Which of these statements is false?

1. Your baby needs complementary feeds until your 'real' milk comes in around day three or four
2. You should weigh your baby before and after feeding to be sure he's had enough
3. Your baby will need solids at four months otherwise he'll be iron-deficient
4. All of the above

2. Breastfeeding beyond 12 months of age is often considered unnecessary. But what do eminent authorities such as World Health Organization recommend?

1. Breastmilk exclusively for first six months
2. Breastfeeding for up to two years and beyond
3. No upper limit to the duration of breastfeeding and no evidence of psychological or developmental harm from breastfeeding into the third year of life or longer
4. All of the above

3. Two hormones that are produced during breastfeeding are designed to make mothering a much easier task. Those hormones are:

1. Oestrogen and progesterone
2. Relaxin and prolactin
3. Oxytocin and prolactin
4. Adrenaline and cortisol

4. Society currently accepts that a 'good' baby is one that sleeps for several hours at a stretch. But how long is the normal sleep-arousal cycle for a young baby?

1. 60 minutes
2. 90 minutes
3. 120 minutes
4. 200 minutes

5. The stress hormones that are produced during the famous fight-or-flight response have adverse effects. What do you know about these hormones?

1. They are adrenaline and cortisol
2. The hormone oxytocin is the direct counter to their effects
3. Babies who are separated from their parents produce higher levels of these
4. All of the above

**Answers**
**Q1:** 1. 1 pt, 2. 1 pt, 3. 1 pt, 4. 4 pts; **Q2:** 1. 2 pts, 2. 3 pts, 3. 3 pts, 4. 4 pts; **Q3:** 1. 0 pts, 2. 1 pt, 3. 4 pts, 4. 0 pts; **Q4:** 1. 0 pts, 2. 4 pts, 3. 0 pts, 4. 0 pts; **Q5:** 1. 2 pts, 2. 2 pts, 3. 2 pts, 4. 4 pts
(The maximum possible score is 20.)

# PART 2:

Life with your toddler and beyond

# CHAPTER 3

## Nurture's the word

### 1. Stimulate all your baby's senses

Everything that your baby sees, smells, hears, touches and tastes is new and fascinating to him and promotes his neurological development.

### 2. Books

It's never too soon to start reading aloud to your baby – it's a chance to provide a different sort of stimulation from what he receives when you wear him, but there are other benefits too.

### 3. Make your baby feel secure

Your baby will be content when he feels like he did when he was in your womb – a good reason to pick him up and hold him close.

### 4. Foster exploration, independence and self-esteem

Try to see the world through your child's eyes.

### 5. The home environment

There's a host of positive things you can do to enhance home surroundings, particularly your child's room when he's ready for separate sleeping quarters.

## 6. Make music

Introduce harmony and rhythm through music – it's never too soon to begin.

## 7. Massage your baby

Learning some simple techniques of baby massage can help you to connect and bond with your baby.

# 1. Stimulate all your baby's senses

Everything that your baby sees, smells, hears, touches and tastes is new and fascinating to him and promotes his neurological development. Multiple connections are created in his brain when all of his senses are stimulated, and the more stimulation he receives, the more he learns! Exposing your baby to the widest possible variety of sights, sounds, textures, tastes and smells will maximise his later ability to comprehend and manage his environment.

Carrying your baby close is a simple way to ensure he receives all those sensations – without overwhelming him. When he's snuggled against your breast or perched over your shoulder he's well aware of everything going on around him, yet he feels safe and secure. It's also impossible to ignore him. When you talk to him and when he feels a part of all your activities in those early months, he automatically experiences a constant stream of sensorial stimulation. Sadly, in modern Western society many babies receive vastly reduced amounts of this sensorial input.

If you put your baby down in a cot, he sees nothing more than the coloured mobile above his head. Tucked away in his nursery, he hears none of your conversations. Lying in his pram, he feels only its monotonous movement and sees an uninterrupted view of a plastic canopy. But at least he might be facing towards you. Think about the new generation of trail-blazing baby buggies that are designed for a jogging mum or dad pushing from behind. You're plugged into your iPod or MP3 player, your baby's screened from the sun or the wind by a strategically draped towel or blanket, and except for the feeling of wheels in motion, he's in a total communication and sensorial vacuum! That vacuum denies him countless opportunities to experience the complete range of sound, sight and movement.

By confining him to a cot, a playpen, a pram or a three-wheeled chariot, you've missed multiple opportunities for stimulation of his touch, position and balance receptors. By tuning in to your listening device rather than offering a running commentary on what you're seeing or feeling, even before he's too young to respond, you're signalling a degree of disconnection from his existence. None of these situations are conducive to the initiation of verbal and non-verbal dialogues that stimulate his vital cognitive processes. Limiting his exposure to sensorial stimulation means that his learning and coordination are compromised from his very earliest days. Your relationship suffers too.

It's no coincidence that in recent years there has been a proliferation of programs aimed at reducing the numbers of clumsy, poorly coordinated children by introducing them to spinning, climbing, tumbling and balancing as well as to music and rhythm activities. These classes are simply replacing the sensorial stimulation that Nature intended all babies to experience.

The answer? Buy a baby sling for your newborn. Practise tying it and imagine settling your baby into it before you hold him in your arms. Then wear it routinely! Share the load too – have your partner take turns with you.

These baby-wearing products now come in gorgeous designer colours, but in so many different configurations. Even the title can be confusing – is it a wrap or a carrier, a shawl, a pack, a pouch or a sling? Some designs have been inspired by women from traditional cultures, others are high-tech Western variations on a traditional theme. Before you make a selection, there are some questions for you to consider. Will you be nursing your baby in the sling? Will you be walking with your baby in the sling? Will your partner be using the sling? What other activities (e.g., housework, sitting at the computer) will you be doing with your baby in the sling?

Indeed, there are lots of things to consider, so I suggest you find friends who wear their babies and try what works for them. If all your friends are stroller-pushing mums, you'll have to find a store where they sell a range and test them for size and suitability. There's a wrap-and-tie type, or a swathe of fabric which drapes over your shoulder and is pulled through a ring, creating a hammock, and these styles might suit your new baby. The wrap and tie needs a little practice to get baby settled – the ring type is simpler – but your older baby might be better in a padded pouch that allows him to face outwards. Adjustable straps can be useful for baby-wearing partners and padding in the straps is essential if you're wearing one for long periods. In the early months your baby's legs should be securely held up, not dangling free.

An older baby who is able to sit up can graduate to a backpack – just make sure it's got padding, adjustable straps and firm support for your lower back. Some styles will include a shade cloth, cushioning for a sleepy head and so on. But whatever your choice, I know you'll almost certainly love the ease and convenience of having your baby close and this is an activity that your partner can happily share. There'll be plenty of opportunities to wheel out that mighty baby chariot when your kids are bigger.

## 2. Books

It's never too soon to start reading aloud to your baby – it's a chance to provide a different sort of stimulation from what he receives when you wear him, but there are other benefits too. Even before he's born you can recite some old-fashioned nursery rhymes. They have simple rhythms that make them ideal for reading out loud, especially if you feel a bit silly reading a more conventional story to your unborn or newborn. Even though they're usually complete nonsense, there's a long oral tradition to most nursery rhymes – a tradition that is in danger of being lost unless parents bring them to life. Try to find a big brightly coloured edition of old favourites.

Building on that tradition, lots of modern children's authors have chosen rhyme and poetry as their medium – accompanied by wonderful illustrations. Reading these stories aloud may even bring back memories from your own childhood – if not, make sure your own child will be able to look back and remember those mad, funny, repetitive rhyming lines. The new authors and their hugely creative illustrators offer a cornucopia of magical stories and pictures for readers and listeners alike. I have fond memories of the books that I read to my boys and, if pushed, can still recite some of them today.

Many books from modern authors will undoubtedly be available to download to your iPad, becoming a movable feast at the touch of a finger on the screen. But even if these offerings delight your child, it's important that you introduce real, printed books and that your child learns to value, respect and treat them with care. Children's books made from real paper are preferable to those with cardboard pages or ones made of plastic – I particularly question the latter material. Who wants to teach their child to submerge a book in the bath or under the hose? If he wants to chew on something, there are better things than books! For the moment, real books will have a role in your child's life – at preschool, school and beyond – so introducing him to the original form of reading is important. And of course ebooks will offer many other reading opportunities down the track. More on the issue of electronic readers in Chapter 6: Be clean and green.

As well as grasping the importance and relevance of books, your child will acquire a number of other skills when he's read to. He'll learn to listen attentively and regular reading sessions will increase his attention span. His vocabulary will grow along with his understanding, not only of words but of the world. Reading books to him will stimulate his imagination in ways that TV and DVDs can never do, since the written word requires both the reader and the listener to conjure up images in their head, rather than have the images created for them.

Here's an early opportunity to show your child what books can really provide. In addition to entertainment, they're a source of information and knowledge about all manner of things. They can take the reader out of the world and transport him to places of wonder and excitement. Books will stimulate questions and conversations. All kids love to be read to – when you do it frequently they'll let you know in no uncertain terms if you miss a word or a page. If you dare to doze off, they'll prod you awake. Be prepared to read the same book again and again, often at the same sitting, or to read one after another – with your child only satisfied when the last word of the last book that he selected has escaped your lips.

Your reading will also lead to conversations and explanations with numerous opportunities to introduce and explain new words or ideas. You'll no doubt be as excited as your child when you see him begin to make the connection between your spoken word and those black marks on the page. Then you can start pointing to the word as he says it . . . Your little reader is on the way to doing it all on his own. Just don't expect to sit back and leave him to his own devices. My boys were both happy to be read to for years after their own reading ability was well established!

Whether your reading exploits with your child result in a bookworm or a reader of a less conventional nature, you can be sure that your child's early exposure to the written and spoken word will leave a positive legacy. Reading to your child is just one early communication opportunity – read on for others.

## 3. Make your baby feel secure

Your baby will be content when he feels like he did when he was in your womb – good reason to pick him up and hold him close. Studies confirm what is fairly obvious – babies cry less when they are carried more, so 'wear' him and get your partner to do so too.

While you're wearing him, you can also use the time-honoured soothing methods of rocking, singing and stroking. Of course rocking your baby happens quite naturally when he's in a baby sling and it's wonderful to see more and more new mums and dads carrying their babies this way. As well as being healthier for your baby's emotional and mental development, at a much more practical level, it leaves both your hands free for other tasks.

Keep in mind that breastfeeding is actually about much more than feeding. It's about pleasure, comfort, security, reassurance, contact and more and therefore knows no schedule, rhyme or reason that you could ever fathom. Become his human 'dummy' for a while. The more responsive you are to him in the early weeks and months, the less clingy and more confident he'll be as he grows – trust me on this. This advice might go against the grain for lots of mums and dads who believe it is their job to make sure their child learns very early on that he can't have their attention whenever he wants it – a strange attitude indeed. At this stage you're his lifeline and the source of all his wellbeing.

As your baby grows older and is able to roll over or creep on his tummy, he'll enjoy being mobile for short periods. But he won't be very happy if he's away from you for too long. When he wants to be reconnected, he'll cry. But by picking him up whenever he does, you definitely aren't spoiling him – you're simply responding to his needs.

Something very positive happens every time that you attend to those cries. Crying is your baby's only means of communicating with you. When he signals, by crying, that he needs something and you immediately pick him up, you're telling him that you care about him and about his feelings. You're also letting him know that he is not completely powerless. Remember what Margot Sunderland says – there are no studies to show that being left to cry is good for babies!

With all his cries answered, your baby starts to experience positive feelings about himself, about the people who care for him and also about his ability to influence his environment. Always remember that your baby does not have 'wants' but only 'needs' and it's your job to meet his needs. It's not possible to 'spoil' him, and to leave his cries unanswered actually goes totally against your instinct as parents.

If you don't believe me, learn how promptly other cultures respond to a crying infant. Hunziker and Barr, writing in 1986 in *Pediatrics*, the journal of the American Academy of Pediatrics, stated that caregivers in 78 per cent of the world's cultures respond quickly to an infant's cries. For instance, the Efe in Africa respond to a baby's cries within ten seconds at least 85 per cent of the time when the baby is between three and seven weeks, and 75 per cent of the time when the baby is 17 weeks old. Kung caregivers respond within ten seconds over 90 per cent of the time during the baby's first three months, and over 80 per cent of the time at one year. But it's the contrast that is so very telling, with American and Dutch caregivers found to be deliberately unresponsive to an infant's cries almost 50 per cent of the time during the baby's first three months!

The same experts who suggest that attending promptly to a crying baby leads to 'spoiling' are likely to suggest 'controlled crying' for the baby who continues to wake through the night. Just remember that your baby's sleep cycle is a mere 90 minutes. He's designed to wake through the night – it's vital for his brain development – so it's an unrealistic expectation for him to do otherwise. He's not trying to make your life miserable. So ignore the advice from the 'let him cry – it's only a habit' brigade. Your baby's needs are real, and those needs are to be close to you, to touch you and to nurse.

Of course it is possible, by ignoring your baby's cries until he realises that they achieve nothing, to suppress his needs. However, those needs haven't gone away. They will surface again later and may not be quite so easily attended to. There is an old Jewish proverb that says 'small children disturb your sleep, large children disturb your lives'. In other words, attend during the early years to your baby's waking, with the most obvious and easiest solution! That child will be less likely to disturb your life when he's older.

If you've ever tried the 'controlled crying' technique, or have watched another mum or dad try it (grandparents are often staunch advocates), you'll know what a churning, uncomfortable feeling those unanswered cries create in your 'other' brains. Nature doesn't make you feel that way without good reason – pay attention to those feelings. By responding immediately to your baby's cries, you're laying the groundwork for trust, respect and completely open lines of communication for all of your parenting years (including those traditionally difficult teenage ones). That's a promise!

Also review 'The family bed' in Chapter 2 for the simplest way to attend to your baby's night-time needs. You can be certain that the night will come when your child will surprise you and will sleep soundly until morning. If you've had him beside you and have enjoyed his softness and his warmth, you may even miss his night-time waking. But you'll also know that you've done your job well and can be confident that you've set him on the way to being a secure and self-confident individual.

## DID YOU KNOW?

Infants in non-Western societies fuss just as frequently as those in Western societies, but due to the prompt response of non-Western mums or other caregivers, the overall cumulative duration of crying is less than what occurs in Western societies.

## 4. Foster exploration, independence and self-esteem

Try to see the world through your child's eyes.

As your baby becomes mobile he'll try to imitate whatever he has seen you, your partner or his siblings do. Once he starts down this path, it's important that you allow him to do whatever he can for himself. To be independent is one of his primary needs and also one of his strongest drives, so be sure to modify his environment so that the need and the drive can be satisfied.

Encourage your toddler's exploration. The activities that appeal to him most are the ones that mean something to him. Obviously these are the ones that he sees those around him do. He'll want to flip the pages of books, open cupboards, take out plates and cups, turn on the stereo or TV, play with your phone, iPad or iPod, put clothes in the washing machine, walk up and down stairs unaided, drive the car, unpack the shopping, vacuum the floor, unlock doors and water the garden. Obviously some of these activities have to be a no-no, but whenever it's appropriate, allow him a chance to try doing these things.

Give him books with real pages in preference to those made of cardboard. Wherever practicable, have an accessible drawer or a cupboard that is free of childproof locks – put only non-destructible, non-harmful items in there that he can pull out (and put back in). Let him press the volume control on the stereo and the start button on the washing machine. Hold his hand while he negotiates the stairs. He can manage a duster or polishing cloth all by himself from a very early age. Let him help with the sweeping or the vacuuming and the watering. Find a small dustpan and brush or broom and a child-size watering-can that he is able to manipulate all by himself. Give him finger foods initially and only a spoon or fork when he is old enough – more on first foods in Chapter 4: Fabulous family food. Get the idea?

Be prepared for his explorations to lead him to the yard or to where there's mud, dirt and water. These expeditions will be enormously interesting and satisfying for him but he'll have no regard for the fact that he will get impossibly dirty or that he might ruin his best clothes. You'll be wise to have as little regard for the mess as your child does and simply remember that skin is very durable and easily cleaned. Don't dress him in fancy outfits for these excursions – instead opt for clothes that can go anywhere including through the 'heavily soiled' cycle of the washing machine.

Let your child feel that he has some mastery over his environment and do nothing for him that he can do for himself. You'll need to help while his fingers and limbs are still small and incompletely coordinated. But give him the chance to repeat each activity until he signals that he's had enough. When you do this, he'll soon master a number of skills and will gain increasing self-confidence with his increasing ability. If you try to see his world through his eyes and appreciate what he's experiencing and how he's feeling, you can lead him to endlessly fascinating discoveries and abilities. Always show him respect and consideration and make him feel that he is a valued and contributing member of your family.

A child who has everything done for him never achieves the satisfying sense of self-worth that comes when he does things for himself. In less developed countries, even the tiniest child is able to contribute in some way to the smooth functioning of his tribe or community. He may collect firewood, gather nuts and berries or herd the livestock. He may simply care for a younger sibling, often doing so when he is hardly bigger than the child for whom he's caring. But no matter how simple the task, whatever he does reinforces his feelings of usefulness and belonging.

The basis of your child's self-esteem is also established in infancy. It begins with the body language that you display. The way in which you hold him, your facial expressions and the tone of voice can all signal that he is loved and valued. When your baby has every cry answered he also knows that you care for him. He feels that he is a worthwhile person. When you enable him to manipulate his immediate environment by doing meaningful things for himself, those positive feelings are constantly reinforced.

All of these positive feelings – love, security and emotional attachment from you and a high degree of mastery over his environment – go a long way to establishing his self-esteem. While it is possible to build a sense of self-worth later in life, it is infinitely more difficult to do so. If the groundwork is firmly laid in infancy and early childhood, self-esteem is almost impossible to undo. It's certainly far easier in those early years to make sure that your child feels really good about himself than it is to try, during adolescence or later, to reverse his poor self-image.

And what of self-esteem? If your child has high self-esteem, then he has something very special. This feeling of self-worth is not a noisy conceit but a quiet and strong sense of his value. A positive feeling of worth will ensure that your child is able to live as a fully functioning member of society. It will determine how he relates to the members of his family, it will influence his choice of friends and how he treats them, it will have a direct bearing on his success at school and in a later career and will be a major influence in the sort of relationships he establishes.

Self-esteem is a factor in your child's future happiness and successes and will also determine how he deals with any failures or unhappiness. It also appears that an individual with high self-esteem not only enjoys better health throughout his life, but lives a longer life as well. Think of other things that are connected to high self-esteem – security, connectedness, uniqueness, assertiveness and competence – and always remember that the family's role in fostering self-esteem is beyond question. If you can give your child this gift in his early years, he will reap the rewards for all his life – and so will you!

## 5. The home environment
There's a host of positive things you can do to enhance home surroundings, particularly your child's room when he's ready for separate sleeping quarters.

The ancient Chinese practice of feng shui can be used to improve the energy of any environment and is now being embraced by more and more Western families and businesses. Below are some of the fundamental feng shui principles for you to consider. If you want to get really serious, consult a practitioner.

For better energy flow in your home, begin by purifying the space before affirming the new energies that you want to welcome. You can then choose the appropriate colours and arrange furniture and other objects in harmonious ways.

## Purify the room

Essential oils such as bergamot, cypress, eucalyptus, clary sage and lemongrass can be used as purifying agents. Burn bergamot and clary sage or lemongrass in an oil burner for an hour each day, for five days before your child is to occupy his room.

You and your partner (and your older children) might also like to compose and repeat some positive affirmations. You can make them specific for your own particular situation.

Here are some possibilities:

- We want peace and love to flow into our home.
- We want health and happiness for our whole family.
- We want this space to be filled with love and laughter.

## Arrange the furniture

When you're arranging furniture in a bedroom, try to imagine how your child will feel from his vantage point (which is usually the bed). Put yourself in his place and think how he'll feel before he falls asleep and when he wakes up – try to create a sense of safety and familiarity. When he's very small, there is no doubt that he'll feel most secure when he sleeps with you – I've already made the case for the family sleeping together. Therefore it's important to ensure that there's a good flow of energy in your own bedroom and that the room is painted in peaceful, calming tones.

When the time comes for your child to move to his own space, the same rules apply. Make sure there are attractive prints or pictures on the walls and that comforting objects, such as favourite toys, books and games, are clearly visible. Place his bed against the wall and opposite the doorway, to create a sense of safety. A bed should be away from a window and not in the middle of the room, since both positions can leave your child feeling exposed. If you have no choice but to place the bed under the window, you could hang a mobile or crystal against the glass. Ideally, bedroom furniture should have smooth, rounded edges and you will create further harmony by putting large, heavy objects close to the floor.

## The paint job

Choose the colours for your child's room according to where the room is positioned and after consulting the pa kua, a simple octagonal figure that indicates different colours and characteristics for eight different compass points. These are a guide to what colour the room, situated in that particular position, should be. A bedroom painted in calming shades and pink, green or lilac would be good choices. Green has the added advantage of promoting creativity. You could select the colour scheme for other rooms according to the following guide.

- North: blue
- North-east: beige
- East: green or brown
- South-east: green
- South: red
- South-west: yellow
- West and north-west: metallic, white or gold

A playroom or study would work best in the north-east corner of the house – this position is associated with knowledge and learning. No room should ever be painted all white or dark blue since these are depressing colours. The use of dynamic, positive yang colours such as red or yellow should be limited, because they can increase the tendency to activity and may interfere with a child's sleep. If consulting a feng shui practitioner, your child's birth date will also be taken into consideration.

## Lighting

Full-spectrum lighting (as in daylight) is used as an essential nutrient by the endocrine system. It is taken into the body largely via the optic nerve and partly through the skin and a lack of it causes stress. Studies have shown that if people are deprived of full-spectrum light – for example if they work in a factory which has only fluorescent lighting – stress indicators such as sick leave go up and productivity goes down. Residents of Northern Hemisphere countries are much more susceptible to a form of depression – seasonal affective disorder – during the long, dark, winter months.

So ensure daylight as much as possible for all your child's activities. Where this is not possible, incandescent light (as in normal light bulbs) is preferable to fluorescent light, which is extremely deficient in the spectrum. It also flickers, which is disturbing to the brain (especially to a child's brain which is developing rapidly until he's about three years old). Unfortunately, environmentally friendly, long-life fluorescent bulbs are no better than the tubes. You may be able to find full-spectrum fluorescent tubes, which are much healthier.

Don't forget that exposure to sunlight is necessary for the manufacture of vitamin D in the skin. More appropriately considered a hormone, vitamin D has been increasingly recognised as a vitally important factor, not only for bone formation, but for total immune competence. In a study published in *Nature Immunology* researchers from the University of Copenhagen found that when T-cells (white blood cells important for immune response) encounter a foreign invader in the bloodstream, they extend a receptor in search of vitamin D. If vitamin D is present, the T-cells become 'activated'. If there is not enough vitamin D in the blood, the cells remain passive and no immune response occurs.

Despite Australia being one of the sunniest countries in the world, one third of the population is vitamin D deficient – thanks in large part to very successful sun-safe campaigns. Sarah Berry ('Slip, slop or scare tactic?', *The Sydney Morning Herald*, 5 April 2012) quotes biochemist and author Lyle MacWilliam who says that the current vitamin D recommendations in Australia are 'seriously out of date'. So limit your child's exposure to the strong midday sun and avoid sunburn, but make sure he gets some regular, unprotected exposure when the sun is more than 50 degrees above the horizon (it's at 90 degrees when it's directly overhead). Vitamin D is manufactured when his skin takes on a very slight pink tinge. There's debate about how quickly vitamin D, which is oil-soluble, is absorbed from the skin with some experts advocating washing with water only. I've never known a kid who wasn't happy to avoid a bath, so use soap on the smelly bits only after your child's time in the sun.

## Order

Try to keep your own and your child's environment in order and reduce muddle and mess where you can. Take a leaf from Maria Montessori's book and give all his toys, books and games a special place on easily accessible shelving in his room. Your child will quickly learn to replace an item from its designated spot (at least that's the theory and it certainly works beautifully in the classroom). He'll also take great pride in doing so. Wherever possible, surround your child with cleanliness, order and beauty and these properties will spill over into his feelings about himself and his life.

## 6. Make music

Introduce harmony and rhythm through music – it's never too soon to begin.

At six months in utero your baby can hear your voice and also responds unmistakably to loud sounds. At the University Paris V in France, Dr Marie-Claire Busnel, Head of Research in the Department of Genetics, Neurogenesis and Behaviour, has investigated foetal hearing. Her findings suggest that unborn babies can distinguish between two syllables and between male and female voices. Further research at the University of North Carolina found foetuses were even able to recognise a story read aloud by their mothers every day for six weeks. Findings such as these have prompted some bizarre attempts to accelerate the rate at which a baby learns. Loudspeakers strapped to the mother's abdomen relaying music, the alphabet and foreign languages have been devised. These devices have not been shown to have any benefits and, in fact, may actually be harmful since overstimulation of some of your baby's developing senses may inhibit the development of others.

But as I've already pointed out, after your baby's born he needs exposure to the world – in all its variety and wonder – to stimulate his brain's development. Since he's able to respond to different sounds in utero, playing music in his immediate environment is a simple way to increase the amount of stimulation he receives. Music also has the ability to soothe, calm, improve mood, increase intelligence and develop memory. There are some small-scale studies linking the playing of Mozart and Bach to an increase in IQ.

When your baby is tiny, sing him some old-fashioned lullabies. These are usually just meaningless rhymes repeated over and over again, but the tone of your voice will comfort and reassure him. Even la-la-la-ing or humming will do, or you might choose to play some short, recorded pieces that last not much longer than five minutes. A solo instrument, with or without a vocal accompaniment, is the best way to begin your child's introduction to music and is preferable to a barrage of indiscriminate, background sound from radio. Full orchestral pieces, while certainly a better choice than morning talkback, can be confusing to young ears. Always keep the volume at a moderate level too, because when your child is very small his hearing is exquisitely sensitive.

As he gets older, you can expand his musical repertoire, although it's still best to keep things relatively simple. When you're travelling in the car, you can play some tapes of those old nursery rhymes or other popular songs that have been performed especially for young children. Sing along! I still fondly recall the words of a host of songs that were part of road trips with little kids.

As your child gets older, you can replace the rhymes with some talking books, poems and more sophisticated melodies. But be aware – these family-centred, in-motor-vehicle forms of entertainment are not to be confused with personalised TV screens in the back seat!

If you're planning to launch a child into Suzuki violin or piano in a few years' time, it's never too early to start playing the requisite tapes or CDs. In fact, the Suzuki method relies on the fact that children can learn to play music in exactly the same way that they learn to speak – after a great deal of listening. Shinichi Suzuki's methods are now followed by thousands of youngsters and their parents around the world. Although many go on to become world-class musicians Suzuki's aim was not to produce musical geniuses, but to nurture the musical talent that is in every child and to provide, through music, the stimulus that will allow the development of other latent talents.

An early introduction to and continuing dialogue with a variety of musical styles is a wonderful way to enhance your child's environment. Of course the time will come when he'll want to choose what he listens to, but if his early years have been full of good music, chances are that he'll continue to enjoy it – along with the rock, dance, hip-hop and heavy metal (at least I live in hope). Don't despair either if a child insists on doing homework while music blares from amplifiers or through headphones – there is good evidence that music has the ability to improve the way the left and right hemispheres of the brain communicate.

Here are some specific suggestions that both infants and older children will enjoy and benefit from:

- Vivaldi's 'Flute Concerto – The Four Seasons'
- Massenet's 'Meditation from Thaïs'
- Bach's 'Jesu, Joy of Man's Desiring'
- Beethoven's 'Piano Concerto 5 (The Emperor Concerto)', Second Movement
- Brahms's 'Symphony No. 3', Second Movement
- Haydn's 'Cello Concerto', Second Movement
- Tchaikovsky's 'Symphony No. 6', Second Movement

## 7. Massage your baby

Learning some simple techniques of baby massage can help you to connect and bond with your baby. Massage stimulates all his touch receptors, getting him used to a full range of movement. Massage also promotes the production of oxytocin. Mothers in traditional societies massage their babies regularly from birth. As your hands move over your baby's body, you'll see and sense him relaxing. What you can't feel or see is his brain becoming denser – the cerebral cortex actually becomes heavier with this sort of stimulation. Your baby will also sense the warmth and caress of your hands and will be likely to return the nurturing when he's old enough.

It's easy to initiate some simple techniques without instruction and if you use them regularly, you'll soon become confident and proficient. This is something that your partner can also learn and enjoy. Choose a regular time for the massage when your baby can sleep soundly after you've finished. Morning is good because you'll both be relaxed for the rest of the day, but leave the massage until at least an hour after you've fed him. It's possible that your baby may want to feed during the session – if so, just do it and then return to his massage later.

Before you begin, you'll need a towel or tissues to wipe up any mess that he makes while he's naked. You'll need some natural nut oil (avoid commercial baby oils which destroy oil-soluble vitamins in the skin). Indian and African mothers favour coconut oil and it certainly has some wonderful health benefits, but whatever you use, make sure it's absolutely pure and organically grown. To stop natural oils from going rancid, you can empty the contents of a vitamin E capsule into the bottle, which should always be dark and made of glass. Warm the oil before you use it by placing the bottle in a container of hot water.

Make sure that the room is also warm enough for your baby to lie naked and that you're comfortable. Sit with something supporting your back and your legs stretched out in front of you. Wear a loose T-shirt and shorts or a skirt that allows your baby to lie on your bare legs. Make sure that your other children are occupied. Now play some relaxing music and begin with your baby on his back. Your touch should be quite firm and should always go from the centre out to the periphery, repeating each movement three times. Start with the chest and follow the sequence of shoulders, arms, hands, abdomen, belly, legs, then feet.

Babies will enjoy this routine from the time they're just a few days old, but be prepared for them still to be lapping it up when they're fully grown. Of course, by then they're well able to return the favour. Their enjoyment of this treatment as young adults is testament to all the calm and connection you've promoted with ongoing oxytocin production throughout their lives.

# NURTURE'S THE WORD:
# TEST YOUR KNOWLEDGE

Now you've learned all about how to nurture your child and promote harmony in the home, you'll find some samples of the *flurishh* learning below. When you've answered the five multiple choice questions that follow, check your scores below. The correct answers to the 250 questions such as these will help you accrue points when you play the *flurishh* game at www.flurishh.com.

1. Stimulation of all kinds is what your baby's brain requires for optimal development. Where is the best place for him to receive appropriate stimulation?

1. In his room surrounded by mobiles, pleasant colours and nursery friezes
2. Outside in his stroller enjoying the fresh air
3. Enjoying nursery rhymes on his mum or dad's lap
4. Worn by mum or dad, in a sling or backpack depending on his age

2. Baby wearing confers a host of benefits. Score one for each correct answer.

1. Warmth and security
2. Sensory stimulation
3. Normal sleep–wake cycle
4. Leaves mum or dad with hands free

3. What do you know about the speed with which different societies respond to a baby's cries?

1. The Efe of Africa respond within ten seconds 85 per cent of time in the baby's first three to seven weeks

2. The Kung of Africa respond within ten seconds 90 per cent of time in the baby's first three months
3. Americans and Dutch respond only 50 per cent of the time in the baby's first three months
4. All of the above

4. Mothers with a very wakeful baby may be told that he isn't wrapped tightly enough or should be left to cry since he'll get used to it. Which of the following statements is true?
1. A newborn baby is designed to wake frequently
2. A newborn baby's sleep cycle is 90 minutes
3. A newborn baby sleeps very lightly and wakes often
4. All of the above

5. The growth and development of your child's brain can be enhanced and supported by multiple positive factors. Those factors include:
1. Stimulation and movement, co-sleeping and frequent breastfeeding
2. Complementary formula with additional DHA and EPA
3. Breastfeeding, baby wearing, co-sleeping, stimulation, nutrition, no toxins
4. Brain development is complete at birth and now nurture takes over

**Answers**
**Q1:** 1. 0 pts, 2. 1 pt, 3. 1 pt, 4. 4 pts; **Q2:** 1. 1 pt, 2. 1 pt, 3. 1 pt, 4. 1 pt; **Q3:** 1. 1 pt, 2. 1 pt, 3. 1 pt, 4. 4 pts; **Q4:** 1. 1 pt, 2. 1 pt, 3. 1 pt, 4. 4 pts; **Q5:** 1. 3 pts, 2. 0 pts, 3. 4 pts, 4. 0 pts

(The maximum possible score is 20.)

# CHAPTER 4

## Fabulous family food

### I. Is your baby ready for solid food?

The answer is definitely 'no' if he's under six months.

### 2. He's reaching for food from your plate?

When that starts to happen, it's really more about exploration than nutrition.

### 3. First foods

Here are some quick and easy suggestions for first foods to try.

### 4. Avoid sugar-overload

Sugar is definitely not 'a natural part of life'.

### 5. Don't rush to wean

The average breastfeeding period worldwide is still more than four years!

### 6. Family meals

Here are some tips on giving your child appetising, interesting food that also provides optimal nutrition for brains, behaviour, bones, teeth, skin, hair and more.

## 7. Make sure your child isn't zinc-deficient

A 1999 University of Queensland study showed that two-thirds of Australian children are zinc-deficient.

## 8. Healthy eating habits for the whole family

Mums regularly tell me that feeding their toddler is their biggest issue. Here is some advice on how to avoid food trauma.

## 1. Is your baby ready for solid food?

The answer is definitely 'no' if he's under six months.

Once, when women and their babies were physically very close for years, breastmilk and breastmilk alone sustained those infants for the better part of their first year of life. Undoubtedly babies would be much better off if this were still the case.

An article published in *Pediatrics*, April 2010, 'The burden of suboptimal breastfeeding in the United States: a pediatric cost analysis', by M. Bartick and A. Reinhold, revealed:

- In the United States the lives of 911 babies could be saved each year if the percentage of mothers who breastfed their infants for the first six months of life rose from about 43 per cent to 90 per cent.
- Increasing the breastfeeding rate would also save $US13 billion a year in medical costs. Researchers conducted a cost analysis of the prevalence of ten common childhood illnesses and the direct costs associated with treating those diseases, as well as indirect costs such as missed time from work.
- Lead author of the paper, Dr Melissa Bartick from Harvard Medical School, said the health benefits linked to breastfeeding had been 'vastly underappreciated'.

When breastfeeding throughout the child's first year was almost exclusive, the introduction of solid food happened as naturally and as easily as eventual weaning. It would certainly be wonderful if every baby had the opportunity to discover food at his own pace in his own time. That's not always an option these days, but if you're prepared to follow your baby's leisurely pace, this is unquestionably the easiest approach for both of you and it's also the healthiest thing for your baby.

If you need to go back to work or if, for some reason, your baby is having formula (either a little or a lot), that shouldn't compromise the chance for your baby's gut to mature fully, nor should it compromise the quality of the food that you offer. However, it will make a difference to the rate at which you present new foods and the means by which you do it. Whether you're able to take the slow approach or need to take a more structured one to introducing food other than breastmilk, there are some important things to keep in mind from the start.

- Your child should always enjoy eating and should be able to participate in the selection of healthy food and, later, in the preparation of healthy meals.
- Mealtimes should be pleasant family times rather than a battleground, times that allow your children to develop healthy eating habits that will last a lifetime.
- You need to look after your own health. If you plan to maintain some level of breastfeeding (night-time and/or early-morning feeds tend to be the last to go), remember the things that you need to ensure an ongoing supply of:
  - whole, unprocessed food
  - robust supplementation
  - plenty of purified water
  - adequate rest
  - minimal stress.

Breastmilk is complete food and drink for at least the first six months of your baby's life. This is true, even in the very hottest weather, and there are no benefits for either you or your baby if you introduce solids before then. In fact, until your baby can sit up, he'll have a hard time dealing with solids as gravity is partly responsible for the movement of food through his gut. Remember all of those eminent bodies that recommend exclusive breastfeeding for at least six months (see Chapter 2: Breastfeeding success).

Contrary to popular opinion, feeding your baby solids isn't likely to get him to sleep through the night – if you're after a minimally disturbed night, you should try sleeping with your baby beside you. If your baby starts early on solid food, it certainly doesn't indicate that he is smarter or more advanced than his peers. His digestive system matures slowly and many of the enzymes required for digestion are totally absent for many months, and if your baby starts on solids before his gut is mature, he runs the very real risk of developing allergies or intolerances. Before six months of age, undigested food particles can be absorbed through the gut wall and this may trigger an inappropriate immune response. These foreign proteins are the triggers for allergies and food intolerances which can result in a range of other difficult-to-resolve physical and mental symptoms.

Babies' guts mature at different rates, and six months is simply an average – just remember that this magical number isn't cast in stone. The health (or otherwise) of the gut microbiota will have a bearing on the rate at which the gut matures. If your baby's intestinal health got off to a less than ideal start, he's a good candidate for later rather than earlier introduction of solids. Go back to 'Better birth in your hands – good nutrition' in Chapter 1 for ways to establish and maintain gut health. The most up-to-date research actually indicates that eight or nine months is probably soon enough to introduce solids, and you can leave it even longer if your baby is showing absolutely no inclination to try finger foods.

After about six months (but the time will vary quite a bit) your baby makes his own secretory IgA, an antibody which coats his intestines and stops the absorption of foreign proteins. This is often also the time when he starts to show real interest in what's on your plate and is also able to manipulate food with his hands. The health of the gut flora also determines production of secretory IgA, another reason to take a premium probiotic product.

Some experts working in the field of clinical ecology recommend that you wait until 12 months before you introduce any of the major allergens to your baby's diet, especially if there's any history of allergy or intolerance in either your own or your partner's family. That means no eggs, wheat, cow's milk products, citrus fruits, strawberries or vegetables from the nightshade family (potatoes, tomatoes, capsicums, eggplants) in the first year of your baby's life. (Peanuts belong on this list too, and although it's unlikely they will be on your infant's menu, peanuts may be an ingredient in commercial products, so be sure to read the labels.) Interestingly, eggs, wheat, dairy and oranges – top of the list of foods that are most likely to trigger an allergic or intolerant reaction – are the foods that clinic nurses have traditionally recommended as 'first foods'. More recently that advice to wait 12 months has been questioned with studies not able to demonstrate unequivocally a reduced incidence of intolerances with late introduction of particularly problematic foods.

So my advice is this: do all you can to strengthen your baby's immune system with good preconception, pregnancy and breastfeeding nutrition, paying particular attention to ensuring an optimally healthy gut with the use of a premium probiotic, then wait until your baby makes a move towards family food. When he does show interest in solids, introduce them one at a time, rotate them and keep an eye out for potential reactions. Be particularly cautious when you're introducing wheat rusks, toast fingers with Vegemite, orange juice and boiled eggs. Forget those poor old peanuts for several years!

## 2. He's reaching for food from your plate?
When that starts to happen, it's really more about exploration than nutrition.

At about six months most babies lose their tongue-thrust reflex. Before this, if you try to introduce solid foods, especially with a spoon, your baby may simply 'push' the food out of his mouth. You might mistakenly assume it's because he doesn't like the taste, so you try another food and another food, endlessly searching for one he likes, when dislike isn't the issue at all.

Ideally, wait until your baby starts to reach for part of your meal himself before giving him food other than breastmilk. Hopefully, by then he'll have some teeth and you'll be able to avoid a lot of work – cooking, pureeing and mashing (and spoon-feeding) – if you give him finger foods to experiment with. He might be closer to eight or nine months before he shows real interest in your lunch or dinner.

If you watch carefully, you'll realise that a lot of what he does is pure and simple experimentation. He's still getting the major part of his nutrition from breastmilk and is now interested in exploring tastes, textures and sensations when he's trying solid food. He may just mouth the food, he might even spit it out. Just relax and rest assured that he's still getting absolutely fabulous nutrition at your breast (assuming, of course, you're following the *Healthy Parents, Healthy Baby* dietary guidelines and taking your supplements!). He'll start to eat when the time is right – and he's the best judge of when that might be! If you look at his nappy, you'll probably see a lot of food is passing through unchanged, confirming that his nutritional rewards from solid meals are still slight.

Since your baby is reaching for food, let him select what he fancies and handle it by himself. His coordination will improve while you're saving time and energy. Obviously some foods are better suited to being picked up by small fingers, so if you can arrange an appropriate selection, he'll not only have fun picking up each item, it's going to be much easier for you. He'll also have fun throwing it away again – that's also part of the experimentation.

Don't become a slave to the preparation of special meals. Your baby will love the opportunity to feed himself and that ability to choose what he wants is a much more positive step than having *your* choice of meal spooned into *his* mouth. Of course into his mouth is not the only place the food will go when he's in charge. It will be all over the floor, his table and chair and in his hair and on his cheeks. Put some newspaper under his feeding station if you're worried about the mess and still give him that breastfeed before you introduce a new food. Nursing him will make sure he's cool, calm and collected (and fed) and ready for his first adventures with family food.

## 3. First foods

Here are some quick and easy suggestions for first foods to try.

In older, traditional cultures it may have been up to two years before babies were offered their first solid food. When that happened, their mothers chewed the food first – their saliva and digestive enzymes overcoming any issue of the baby's immature digestive system. If you're not up for pre-masticating your baby's food, start with the low-reactive things – banana, papaya or pear are good options. Your baby may need help if he's only six months old – mash a little of the food and offer it on a spoon. Older babies can handle a slice or a strip of whatever. But when introducing anything new, always be on the lookout for signs of sensitivity or intolerance – gut problems, skin problems, runny nose, earache, unusual or excessive crying – you know by now how your baby looks and behaves so it should not be hard to spot a change. The best way to be sure that a particular food is not causing a problem is to give one food at a time. In a meal of multiple ingredients it's much harder to identify the offending one.

If a particular food does cause a mild reaction, stop it and try it again a month or two later when your baby's gut has matured. Always be guided by your baby – if he always reacts adversely, leave it alone. If he flatly refuses to eat one particular food consistently, while accepting plenty of others, he may know more about his body's ability to digest or tolerate it than you do.

## Offer plenty of variety

Don't give the same old foods meal after meal, day after day. Together with solids that were introduced too early, constant and frequent exposure has a great deal to do with the development of allergies and intolerances.

Introduce raw vegies early – celery and carrots are good. But be sure to keep your eye on those early forays into chewing and swallowing. If anything gets stuck in your child's throat, or goes down the wrong way, put him over your knee, head lower than chest and tap sharply several times between his shoulderblades.

Don't overdose your baby on fruit. The sugar content is high and he needs to try other foods as well. Best practice is to avoid strawberries and citrus fruits until well past six months (while some experts suggest 12 months) and always be aware of the possibility of an adverse reaction.

With both fruit and vegetables you'll need to get rid of the external undesirables. Spray with apple cider vinegar, then rinse well with running water. You can peel the vegetable or fruit if the skin is tough and your baby is very young. But don't forget that lots of the vitamins and minerals are just under the skin. Also, remember that organic produce is best. If you think organic is too expensive, compute the extra nutritional value and the absence of toxicity into your family's long-term health equation; the value of organic produce will definitely be seen in both the short and much longer term! That simple step of shopping at an organic supplier will reduce your child's exposure to potentially harmful pesticides and other chemicals by a significant amount! Vary the texture and taste of raw vegies by dipping them in a simple vinaigrette dressing. You'll find recipes in the 'In your kitchen' section of this book and *Healthy Parents, Healthy Baby*.

A chop bone or chicken drumstick can serve as your baby's introduction to meat. Fish is a wonderfully nutritious food for children – all those omega-3s for their brains and eyes from the deep-sea varieties. Try different varieties of fresh fish – save the canned varieties for emergencies.

Yoghurt is very easily digested, provides protein and calcium and can be mixed with sweet or savoury foods, but you should avoid the commercial varieties that are often sweetened with sugar and contain emulsifiers and thickeners – stick to the natural ones or better still, make your own.

Keep away from the 'big grasses' such as wheat, rye and barley until your baby is older. Instead, look to some of the other grains to prepare nutritious mueslis or porridges. Try brown rice, buckwheat, millet, quinoa and couscous but be sure to cook them well.

Eggs – victim of terrible press for many years – are an absolutely fabulous food, a great source of protein and many essential nutrients. However, they are a common cause of intolerance, so they're definitely another food to leave for later and watch their introduction carefully. Remember of course that the best eggs will come from hens that have been organically fed and free to roam. Read labels very carefully; pictures on packaging can often be misleading and conditions on free-range farms can vary, so look for accreditation details from a reputable organisation.

## What about drinks?

While breastmilk was your baby's only source of food and fluid, you didn't have to worry about his hydration needs. Now you'll need to give your toddler an alternative thirst quencher and for that purified water can't be beaten. If you haven't already invested in a filter for your drinking water, this is the time to do so. (For more details see 'Wet, weird and wonderful water' in *Healthy Parents, Healthy Baby*.) Remember, an older child really doesn't require another form of milky drink. Avoid commercial fruit juices too – you can make your own fresh juices to add variety to the drinks menu if you want. Don't give fluids just before or at mealtimes as they'll fill that little tummy really quickly and dilute digestive juices.

On the subject of small tummies, three solid meals a day may not be in your child's best interests simply because he doesn't have the storage capacity for large amounts of food. Offer grazing opportunities, small frequent snacks and nothing that needs to be specially prepared.

If there are times when you have no option but to use pre-prepared baby foods, choose organically grown and free from pesticides and other additives. A lot of commercial products contain gluten, cow's milk, sugars and fillers and possibly GM produce as well, so check those labels carefully.

## DID YOU KNOW?

In 2011, the *Journal of Epidemiology & Community Health* reported that children who eat a nutritious diet of fruits and vegetables have higher IQ levels, while a diet of processed and sugary foods has the opposite effect. The Avon Longitudinal Study of Parents and Children, which tracked around 14,000 children for five years, showed that greatest benefits are seen when a child starts early on a healthy diet, and especially during the first three years.

## 4. Avoid sugar-overload

Sugar is definitely not 'a natural part of life'.

That said, it can be challenging to avoid when most of us wage a constant battle with our 'sweet tooth' and when sweets are so closely associated with pleasure, treats and rewards – and yes, even breastmilk is sweet!

Our natural tendency to favour a sweet flavour may be traced back to an evolutionary adaptation when we discovered that the consumption of fruit (sweet) gave us more energy than grazing on grass or chomping on leaves. Having more energy gave us a break from our need to be constantly in search of a supply of green fodder, leaving us free to get on with the business of being human – making tools, developing weapons, painting cave art and so on . . . Urban myth or true story – who knows for sure? But it's a good tale, and the bottom line is sweet tastes are inherently pleasing.

Today our sugar consumption is approaching a massive 60 kilograms per person per year. Equivalent to more than half a cup of refined sugar each day, that consumption isn't coming primarily from natural, unrefined sources, either; to do so, you would need to eat about 1 kilogram of sugar beet or consume several metres of sugar cane! Crucially, the over-consumption of sugar has been linked to obesity, diabetes and other chronic conditions.

Food manufacturers must be held to account – they add increasing amounts of sugar to processed foods, including to unlikely items such as tomato sauce and soup, as well as create ever more palatable products using sugar to camouflage what would otherwise be totally unpalatable. I've written at length about the problems of over-consumption of sugar-laden products in every single one of my books, in particular *Healthy Parents, Healthy Baby* and *The Natural Way to Better Breastfeeding*, but here is a summary of the most important points.

- The brain controls mood, mind, memory and behaviour.
- The brain also controls hormones, breathing rate, motor activity, sense perception and more.

- The brain uses only glucose, a simple sugar, to fuel all its functions, but this simple sugar does not come from consumption of simple sugars.
- The brain requires a steady supply of glucose to function optimally.
- Glucose molecules are formed by the breakdown of complex carbohydrates.
- Complex carbohydrates are found in grains, in legumes and varieties of beans, as well as in abundance in fruit and vegetables.
- Complex carbohydrates are broken down to glucose over a period of hours.
- That means glucose reaches the brain at a steady rate and all brain functions can proceed normally.
- Refined sugar (essentially pre-digested complex carbohydrates) is broken down to glucose in minutes.
- High circulating levels of glucose in the blood stimulate insulin production.
- Insulin takes the circulating glucose out of the bloodstream and stores it in the liver as glycogen (or later converts it to fat).
- Now there is too little circulating glucose.
- When the brain receives too much or too little fuel, the organ and all the functions under its control are compromised.
- Your child's brain develops rapidly until about three years of age, so it is particularly affected.
- A child is also susceptible to fluctuating glucose levels since he may consume a relatively large amount of sugar for his small body weight.
- He will exhibit an array of responses depending on his individual make-up. Irritable, cranky, defiant, anxious, whiny, sleepy, unable to concentrate, poorly coordinated – the list of subtle or blatantly obvious effects is long. You might simply

think he is just tired, careless or bored, shrugging it off as life with a toddler.

- But whatever the symptoms, he'll now be looking for another sugary snack because it will temporarily make him feel better and the cycle starts again.

- Party fare is notorious for precipitating this type of behaviour. Soft drinks, large quantities of pure fruit juice and going too long without a snack or a meal can all do the same.

Refer to *Healthy Parents, Healthy Baby* for all the details about balancing protein, carbohydrate and healthy oils in the right proportions so that poor blood sugar control doesn't send your child off the rails.

One final word of warning: as well as avoiding foods that contain sugar (remember lots of the other names for sugar end in '-ose'), be particularly careful to avoid high-fructose corn syrup (HFCS), used increasingly in processed food. It appears that the metabolic pathway for the breakdown of this member of the sugar family differs from the already described pathway to glucose, with research showing that diets containing equivalent caloric amounts of sucrose and HFCS are definitely not equivalent in their ability to cause weight gain, increase body fat and blood lipids and precipitate the development of 'metabolic syndrome'. In 2010 researchers at Princeton University found that high-fructose corn syrup prompted considerably more weight gain in lab animals. 'These rats aren't just getting fat; they're demonstrating characteristics of obesity,' said graduate student Miriam Bocarsly. 'In humans, these same characteristics are known risk factors for high blood pressure, coronary artery disease, cancer and diabetes.' Suffice to say, HFCS is an absolute no-no!

## 5. Don't rush to wean

The average breastfeeding period worldwide is still more than four years!

If you're comfortable with infant-led weaning – after all, what easier way for both you and your baby – you might be breastfeeding for several years (and that's just for one child). Think of the time and energy you'll save if you offer the breast when that's what your baby wants and then let him help himself to the appropriate parts of your family meal. If you're determined to breastfeed until your child tells you he's had enough, be prepared to ignore the prophets of doom who'll predict that you'll be offering your breast through the university gates. Briefly, there are enormous benefits for both you and your baby, so adopt the attitude that your baby knows best and just keep nursing.

I'm a big fan of infant-led weaning – it's just so simple! One day your breastfeeding toddler doesn't come for his early-morning feed and it's done, or a suggestion that he might find another activity more interesting can have the same effect. The absolute certainty is that your child will wean himself when he's good and ready – whenever that might be. That moment will be entirely up to his unique physical, mental and emotional clock, free from individual or society's prejudices or other constraints.

This point was reinforced to me recently when my extremely articulate 20-year-old was interviewed by Dr Rosina McAlpine for her book *Inspired Children: How the leading minds of today raise their kids*. Mikey was still breastfed when he went to preschool, alone among his classmates, and continued for a good while after. However, in response to Rosina's question, he said, 'It just felt absolutely normal to me.' Trust that your child is the expert when it comes to weaning.

I'd love to see every baby breastfed for at least two years because I know how much healthier and happier our children would be. That said, I'm a pragmatist. If you've decided that you've had enough, then here are some tips for making weaning as stress-free as possible.

## Gradual weaning

Gradual weaning is best for your baby – it gives his digestive system time to adapt to new foods. He also needs to develop some new food- and drink-handling skills. If you're weaning after nine or ten months, avoid a bottle and go straight to a sippy cup, heeding the advice on safest plastics in Chapter 6: Be clean and green.

Gradual weaning is best for you too – it allows your milk supply the chance to adapt and reduces the risks of engorgement and mastitis. 'Gradual' means eliminating feeds one at a time. Early-morning or late-evening feeds could continue on for a while, and always remember your breast can provide a comfort stop that your child will still enjoy. As I mentioned in Chapter 2, breast versus bottle need not be an either/or choice.

## Infant formula

If your baby is weaned from the breast before purified water becomes a viable alternative as a drink, low-reactive milk formula, available from your pharmacy, is the best product to use.

## Cow's milk

Weaning an older child doesn't mean replacing breastmilk with cow's milk. Cow's milk (at least the pasteurised variety) is the most common allergen and calcium, iron and other nutrients are poorly absorbed from cow's milk, despite the aggressive marketing campaigns by dairy farmers. Two-thirds of the world's population get their calcium requirements from non-milk sources, such as cultured yoghurt (better tolerated than milk or cheese by most people), green leafy vegetables and fish such as salmon and sardines (with the bones). Try goat's milk if you really want to give your child a milky drink.

Raw, unpasteurised milk is another alternative, but unless you live on a farm, your chances of getting it are slim. While many physicians of Dr Weston Price's day (the 1930s) studied the significant health-promoting properties of raw milk for children (and many animal studies confirm its benefits over pasteurised milk), the regulatory bodies are adamant that it will not be available to consumers today.

## Soy

With pasteurised milk and formula based on cow's milk proving to be unsuitable for lots of infants, and raw milk an unobtainable option, soy-based formula seemed like the answer to the prayers of mums wanting a milk drink for babies. Sadly, the reality has turned out to be equally problematic – with massive increases in consumption leading to a generation of kids who are allergic to soy.

Soy infant formula contains a class of compounds called isoflavones, which are phytoestrogens. These compounds are found in plants and can act like the hormone oestrogen in the body. Infants go through developmental stages that are sensitive to oestrogens, which is why some authorities recommend no soy formula before 24 months, since the long-term effects of giving soy to infants is unknown. As well, soy, which is a secondary protein, fails to provide all the essential amino acids and also contains phytates that can block the absorption of proteins and essential minerals. Worse still, some soy brands may be high in sugar and may contain genetically modified beans and even aluminium, which is a toxic metal and a burden for immature kidneys.

## Fruit juice

Commercial fruit juices contain the sugar of tens of apples, oranges or pears and their consumption has been linked to dental decay and chronic non-specific diarrhoea. Juices dilute the hydrochloric acid in the stomach and thus reduce the absorption of nutrients. They suppress appetite for other food. Juices also establish a habit of reaching for sugar-containing products to quench thirst when water is all that's required.

Yikes – why ever would you be searching for an alternative to breastmilk? Who needs to fuss about any of this? Just keep breast-feeding! When your child does come off the breast, introduce him to water. Purified water, as a thirst quencher, can't be beaten. Setting a water-drinking example yourself will help. Homemade fruit smoothies prepared with an overripe banana, some unsweetened yoghurt and water can make a change from what comes from your water filter. You can always vary the flavour by using a different variety of fruit. Freshly squeezed vegetable juices are another occasional drink option. See 'In your kitchen' for some suggestions.

### DID YOU KNOW?

Researchers say that baby and infant formula and foods are full of toxins that could cause inflammation and diabetes later on in life.

## 6. Family meals

Here are some tips on giving your child appetising, interesting food that also provides optimal nutrition for brains, behaviour, bones, teeth, skin, hair and more.

If you have nursed your child through his toddler years, the period following complete weaning may be the most difficult of all when you're trying to feed him a healthy diet. While your baby and toddler is entirely at your mercy in terms of what you give him, an older child has a voice of his own and unique likes and dislikes as well. He may also be exposed to a great deal of advertising and be influenced by what his peers are eating. Demands for inappropriate food and drink can be quite insistent and can wear you down (especially when you're trying to juggle the demands of home, work and other children). But don't just throw up your hands and give in. Eating a healthy diet is more important than ever before, because your child's nutritional needs are no longer met completely by your breastmilk.

## Nutrients for brain function

Even when your child's brain development is pretty much complete, its correct function still depends on an adequate supply of essential nutrients. Research indicates that the required nutritional intake for optimal intellectual development may actually be far in excess of those levels that appear necessary to maintain physical health. Numerous studies show that children consuming the 'average Western diet' but given a modest vitamin and mineral supplement exhibit improved intellectual functioning that can be measured by various scoring methods. Remember, too, the study mentioned above which showed higher IQ levels in those children whose diets contained lots of vegetables and fruit.

## Nutrients for strong bones and teeth

Your child needs an adequate nutritional intake to meet all aspects of his rapid physical growth and development, even though this rate slows considerably after his first year of life. Bones continue to grow and their density is determined by the diet that your child eats now. A diet high in soft drinks and processed foods means reduced bone density due to increased excretion of calcium. This means a greater chance of fractures at the very time your child is learning to climb trees, ride a bike and play sport. If your young daughter's diet doesn't ensure strong bones are laid down in her youth, she risks osteoporosis after menopause. (The other factor to remember here is the positive effects of weight-bearing exercise on bone density.)

Second teeth are forming during these years and zinc as well as calcium is important for their formation. Zinc deficiency is a contributing factor in very late teething and second teeth that are slow to erupt. Adequate zinc status also gives your child bright eyes, glossy hair and appropriate taste sensation; by contrast, a deficiency means dull, dry, lack-lustre hair and a tendency to eat only very sweet or salty foods. Zinc and vitamin C are needed for healthy skin, which in optimum condition is actually remarkably resistant to the damage caused by minor bumps and scrapes. The skin damage caused by more serious accidents will heal quickly and is unlikely to become infected when your child's nutritional status is sufficient. More on zinc below.

## Nutrients for body function

Some of the benefits of a healthy diet may not be so apparent. A diet that is low in fat and high in fibre and all essential nutrients is also important for proper digestion, for easy and regular elimination and for a fully functioning immune system. It can reduce the risk of atherosclerosis, arthritis, diabetes and cancer in adulthood, and it can ensure sound mental function and much more. Finally, it can affect your child's future fertility and reproductive health and ultimately the health of your grandchildren.

Lots of compelling reasons to ensure meals are full of whole foods and packed with all the nutrients your family needs, and the 'In your kitchen' section gives you plenty of ideas on how to do it!

## 7. Make sure your child isn't zinc-deficient

A 1999 University of Queensland study showed that two-thirds of Australian children are zinc-deficient. Meanwhile, World Health Organization estimates that up to 80 per cent of Western society may be zinc-deficient.

I actually believe we have an epidemic of conditions related to zinc deficiency in those kids conceived directly after years of oral contraceptive use by their mums. You can read more about the zinc-depleting effect of the Pill and other lifestyle factors in *Healthy Parents, Healthy Baby*. Looking at the results of the University of Queensland study, I suggest that much of the observed zinc deficiency in children has its beginnings in utero. But how does that deficiency play out in children?

Zinc is necessary for proper brain formation and function, a competent immune system, and the formation of testicular tissue (boys need five times more zinc than girls for their development). Also, babies with adequate zinc status are easy to settle. Yet we see increasing numbers of children with learning and behavioural problems and allergies to all manner of things. Undescended testes is now so common that it is no longer a notifiable condition and far too many babies are jittery and hard to console.

Also, consider zinc's role in taste and smell sensation. Children who will eat only very salty or very sweet food are often zinc-deficient; more subtle flavours (such as those of fruit and vegetables) are lost on them. What's more, the late chemistry professor Derek Bryce-Smith, at the University of Reading, UK, showed that 80 per cent of anorexics are zinc-deficient. It goes without saying that when food tastes like cardboard, it's easy to refuse. Zinc deficiency also affects brain function, distorting body perception so that the food-refusing individual does not see the true extent of their rake-thin frame. Do you recognise the combination? We now have an epidemic of young women (and more and more young men) suffering from anorexia – a condition that was relatively unknown 40 years ago. Zinc supplementation is also useful in the treatment of anxiety and depression – other mental health issues that are reaching epidemic proportions.

Zinc is necessary for wound healing – so it's a pretty important nutrient in a toddler's world where bumps and scrapes are frequent. Zinc, along with other trace elements, is also involved in creating healthy hair, bones and teeth, it's vital at puberty for optimal growth and is also necessary for muscle-building.

If you think your kids could do with some zinc, look for white spots on their fingernails or test your own status, which will give you a good idea of theirs if they're too young to undertake the test. You'll find all the details about the Zinc Taste Test and zinc-rich foods for your shopping list in *Healthy Parents, Healthy Baby*.

## DID YOU KNOW?

A 2011 study by researchers from the University of New South Wales found that one in ten children cannot identify food as being sweet, salty, bitter or sour. The prevalence of taste disorders in Australian children is three times the level acceptable to World Health Organization and needs urgent attention, say the researchers.

## 8. Healthy eating habits for the whole family

Mums regularly tell me that feeding their toddler is their biggest issue. Here is some advice on how to avoid food trauma.

First let me ask you . . .

- Why do children reject some foods?
- If they don't like a particular food, why will they hold it in their mouth and refuse to swallow?

- How do children learn to dislike?
- Why are rewards for eating counterproductive?
- Why is forced eating very counterproductive?

The answer to all these questions lies in the biological defence mechanisms children naturally have against eating something that might not be safe to eat. Children will only freely eat what they are familiar with and have confidence in eating.

So where does that confidence begin? We know that the mother's eating habits in utero will determine whether her child favours unhealthy or healthy food. We also know that a mum who eats cruciferous vegetables (that's broccoli, cauliflower, cabbage and brussels sprouts) when she's pregnant will give her child lifelong protection from cancer – even if the child never eats those vegies again.

Furthermore, breastfeeding mums who eat a wide variety of healthy food will establish a tendency for their child to be more adventurous when it comes to new tastes and textures. Obviously a great deal of taste and inherent preference for healthy over unhealthy food has taken place before your child even reaches across the table to make a selection. However, even though you may have made some positive early steps doesn't mean you're off the hook just yet!

Let's now review some of the factors that can lead to fabulously happy and healthy family mealtimes and, if you're really lucky, to kids who eventually take the initiative in your kitchen!

## Pregnancy and breastfeeding habits

- It starts in pregnancy – your baby will be more likely to enjoy the foods you ate during pregnancy, so make wise choices.
- The foundations for a child who enjoys variety, who appreciates subtle tastes and who will tend to choose healthy options in preference to junk food are set in motion during your baby's months in utero.

- Continue a healthy and varied diet while you're breastfeeding and guess what – your baby is likely to follow suit.
- A variety of flavours in breastmilk makes a baby more accepting of new flavours when he starts to eat solid foods.

Of course the converse holds true. In any family, bad habits are more contagious than measles!

What are you and your partner eating?

## Set an example

- If nothing fresh, green or alive ever passes your lips, then don't expect your children to tuck into broccoli and brussels sprouts with relish.
- If you snatch a croissant with jam for breakfast, then it's unlikely that your children will be found happily spooning up their oatmeal.
- If you frequently consume drinks that come from a can or bottle, it's going to be difficult to get your children to drink the water that comes free from the filter.
- Studies show that it is the father's eating habits that the child will mimic – a pretty heavy responsibility for all you dads!

## You're a role model but also in control

- Remember that when your child is very young, you have complete control over what he eats. Good eating habits can be firmly established in those early years.
- You can help your toddler recognise what is healthy and what is not. You can explain how food is grown, how it is processed, added to and so on.
- Try taking him to organic markets and make the comparison between what's there and what's on the supermarket shelves.

- Explaining to him the reasons for avoiding refined and processed products may help him to resist peer pressure and make good choices when he's older. Even if he strays for a while, chances are excellent that his taste for real, healthy food will get him back on track eventually.
- Promote new foods as interesting and exciting.
- Expect acceptance, not refusal.
- If new foods are refused, just acknowledge it as a natural safety mechanism.
- Don't force a child to eat – but do try reintroducing the food later.
- Trust him when he says, 'I've had enough.'

## Set aside the time to eat

- You might have noticed that whole, unrefined foods take more time to chew. This means you can't bolt down a nourishing meal in the same time you can demolish a burger with fries.
- Once your child is eating vegetables and brown rice, even though he may be able to feed himself, some degree of supervision at mealtimes is helpful.
- The added time taken to chew, and therefore finish a meal, means that boredom may set in before fullness.
- This is when eating together as a family is important – conversations, and sometimes books, puzzles or otherwise interesting activities for the younger child, are a means of keeping the child at the table until he's eaten his fill.
- Make sure that older children aren't allowed to leave the table until everyone is finished. It's not only good manners, but it may lead to productive family interaction and your baby will certainly enjoy the company.
- Which brings me to another issue – a baby sitting alone in a highchair to eat all by himself has no good example to follow.

## Supplements

- If you're still breastfeeding and supplementing appropriately, your toddler will get his zinc through your breastmilk. Don't give zinc as a single nutrient.
- In addition to zinc, add a well-balanced multivitamin and mineral supplement designed for children. Even if your child's zinc levels are okay, regular nutritional supplementation has lots of benefits. In particular, ensure a good source of omega-3s, such as krill oil, from a sustainable source, for brain and eye development and function.
- A probiotic for children, or better still a premium yoghurt manufactured from a culture of human-only strains, should also be included in your growing child's daily diet to help ensure a healthy gut – the foundation for optimal physical, mental and emotional wellbeing.

### DID YOU KNOW?

A 2007 study by the NSW Centre for Overweight and Obesity showed mothers were more concerned about their children being underweight than overweight and many unnecessarily battled to get them to eat.

In summary, remember your child's diet should be essentially the same as the one you've been following for healthy conception, pregnancy and breastfeeding.

## Eat more of these

- ✓ Organically grown (or raised in the case of animal produce)
- ✓ Whole, fresh and unrefined
- ✓ Prepared from scratch
- ✓ Vegetables and fruit
- ✓ Whole grains

✓ High-quality protein (if you're vegetarian, combine different types of vegetable protein)

✓ Mono-unsaturated oils (e.g., olive oil). Coconut oil is another good choice for cooking at high temperatures

✓ Plenty of purified water

## Get rid of these

✗ Refined 'white' foods or those containing white flour, sugar or sugar substitutes

✗ Additives (includes almost everything in a packet, can or bottle. Colourings and caffeine are of particular concern)

✗ Products containing hormones or antibiotics

✗ Saturated fats (including animal fats, fried foods and margarine)

✗ Delicatessen meats – high in fat, salt, nitrates and nitrites, which are carcinogens

✗ Common table salt

Following these recommendations will give you the best chance of enjoying happy family mealtimes. They'll set the foundation for a child with a healthy body and a fully functioning brain. They are also environmentally sound eating habits, and ones that your child will pass on to his children when the time comes. Most importantly, they won't leave your child with memories of food trauma!

# FABULOUS FAMILY FOOD:
# TEST YOUR KNOWLEDGE

Now you've learned all about healthy eating habits for all the family, you'll find some samples of the *flurishh* learning below. When you've answered the five multiple choice questions that follow, check your scores below. The correct answers to the 250 questions such as these will help you accrue points when you play the *flurishh* game at www.flurishh.com.

1. Choose the statement that most closely reflects your understanding of modern agricultural practices.
1. Non-sustainable farming practices lead to nutrient-poor produce
2. We are better nourished because of modern farming practices
3. My nutritional mantra: healthy whole food grown on healthy soil
4. Modern farming practices mean less likelihood of food-borne disease

2. Choose the correct statements as they relate to how your baby's gut is inoculated with healthy gut bacteria. Score one for each correct answer.
1. As he passes down the birth canal
2. Not if he's born by caesarean section
3. As he breastfeeds
4. Not if he's bottle-fed

3. Nutrient losses occur when vegetables are transported, stored and cooked. Which of the following preparation methods produce the least amount of nutrient loss?
1. Dry-baking
2. Steaming
3. Stir-frying
4. Raw where possible. I avoid boiling, deep-frying and particularly avoid microwaving

4. Which of the following statements about sugar are true?
1. Sugar is an ingredient in products such as tomato sauce
2. Sugar is a natural part of life
3. Current sugar consumption is about 10 kilograms per person per year
4. Foods containing sugar, especially high-fructose corn syrup (HFCS), should be avoided

5. A zinc-deficient toddler may suffer from which of the following . . .
1. Poor taste perception – eating only very sweet or salty food
2. Compromised immunity, chronic illness and learning or behavioural problems
3. Delayed teething, slow wound healing and poor growth
4. All of the above

**Answers**
**Q1:** 1. 3 pts, 2. 0 pts, 3. 4 pts, 4. 0 pts; **Q2:** 1. 1 pt, 2. 1 pt, 3. 1 pt, 4. 1 pt; **Q3:** 1. 1 pt, 2. 1 pt, 3. 1 pt, 4. 4 pts; **Q4:** 1. 2 pts, 2. 0 pts, 3. 0 pts, 4. 2 pts; **Q5:** 1. 2 pts, 2. 2 pts, 3. 2 pts, 4. 4 pts
(The maximum possible score is 20.)

# CHAPTER 5

## The magic of movement

### 1. Get your child moving

Sadly, in today's society, lack of physical activity can begin at birth. Start with some basic exercises early and you'll set the foundation for a lifetime of physical activity.

### 2. Ways to encourage activity

It's easier to begin early, encouraging good exercise habits, than it is to try to prise a slothful teenager off the lounge.

### 3. Exercise as a family

Do you wonder how you'll find the time or the energy to exercise? It might surprise you, but you'll actually find that you have more of both when you make exercise a regular part of your day.

### 4. Yoga for kids

Another way to shape your child's attitude to movement and exercise, as well as to life in general, is to introduce him to yoga.

### 5. Competitive sports

These days, a great deal of activity for children is very structured and is based around competitive team sports. But when it comes to competitive sports, there are some important considerations.

## 6. Travel with kids

'Harmony' and 'travelling with children' need not be mutually exclusive.

## 1. Get your child moving

Sadly, in today's society, lack of physical activity can begin at birth. Start with some basic exercises early and you'll set the foundation for a lifetime of physical activity.

These days, from the time many children are born, they are immobilised in a car seat, a pram or a stroller, a cot or a bouncer and receive little of the stimulation that would indicate constant movement as a normal and desirable part of life. This confinement also sets the stage for a child who's happy to lie on the sofa watching TV, to sit in front of computer or video games for endless hours, or one that is simply happy to observe from the sidelines – an innocent bystander in the game of life. You can counter this pattern of inactivity early to ensure that your child becomes a participant! When your baby is tiny, you can begin the stimulation of his muscles by doing some very simple exercises, outlined below. These can be done straight after his massage and are designed to accustom developing muscles to movement and to improve coordination.

- Begin by holding your baby's hands in yours – open his arms out to the sides. Now fold his arms across his chest, right over left. Repeat the sequence, this time folding left over right. Repeat three times on each side.
- Now take your baby's right hand and left leg in your hands and gently extend them, then fold them in to meet one another. Swap hands and extend his left hand and right leg, before bringing them in and folding them over one another. Repeat this sequence three times on each side. This is a good exercise for improving coordination.
- Hold your baby's right leg, with the knee bent, against your thigh. Now bend his left leg up towards his tummy. Reverse the sequence and repeat three times on each side. Now bend both your baby's legs up to his tummy – first do right over left

as in the lotus position, then repeat with left over right. Repeat this sequence three times.

These are just a sample of the exercises that you can do with your baby. As he grows stronger and accustomed to them, you can add others.

There are other simple ways to encourage activity – and I outline some of these in greater detail in the following section. But for now it's important to understand just why movement matters!

In earlier eras, and still in some cultures today, children were, and still are, carried in a way that ensured familiarity with the sensation of constant motion. Nature has devised a truly perfect system. If you carry your infant in your arms or close to your body, he'll automatically be exposed to a full range of movement and to all sorts of other sensations as well.

When your baby is carried close he receives the tactile stimulation of your body's movement against his. His specialised sensory receptors, called proprio-receptors, receive signals that tell him about the position of his body, which way it is aligned and its size and shape. As you move, the vestibular mechanisms in his inner ears are stimulated – which is vital for his balance and for the integration of all those messages he receives from his eyes, nose, ears, skin and other sensory receptors. Continual sensorial input primes your child for later activity. It enhances his coordination and fosters development of his spatial judgement. Think writing skills, aptitude for ball games, sporting prowess in a host of different areas, driving skills (down the track, of course) and much more. That stimulation also sends him a very important message. He learns that life is all about movement – it's not about lying or sitting still.

## 2. Ways to encourage activity
It's easier to begin early, encouraging good exercise habits, than it is to try to prise a slothful teenager off the lounge. Begin by carrying your baby close.

## Wear your baby

If children are to regain familiarity with movement, your baby should be 'worn' – which simply means being carried close in his early months. First of all, carry him in a baby sling or snuggly, making sure that those little legs are tucked up and well supported by the fabric.

Once his core is strong enough and he can sit up, a backpack will be more comfortable for you. Backpacks for toddlers are constructed in exactly the same way as the most sophisticated hiking and mountaineering equipment, with adjustments and padding to take the strain off your shoulders and make the experience comfortable for the small passenger as well.

So keep your baby close as you go about your daily activities. Wear your baby around the house, or as you walk to the shops or to school with your other children. If you need an added incentive, think of the extra work-out that you'll get – there'll probably be little need for other forms of exercise! Of course, both you and your partner need to be strong and fit to 'wear' your baby – go back to my recommendations in *Healthy Parents, Healthy Baby*, Chapter 4: Do.

Wearing your baby can take the stress out of trying to return to your pre-baby levels of physical activity. Remember, there are lots of different ways to be active and also remember that if there are days when you simply don't have the inclination or the energy, then it's okay to leave it for tomorrow – just as long as that 'tomorrow' doesn't get put off to become 'never'.

## Crawling and exploring

The need for movement continues throughout your toddler's early years. Once, a child was free to crawl and to learn about his world by putting objects in his mouth, squeezing them between his fingers and toes and rubbing them in his hair. These exploratory activities always took place within the safe confines of villages or homes where adults and older children were constantly present and aware of what the smaller child was doing. But these days, when extended families are a thing of the past, when busy schedules conspire against parents' patience for such leisurely explorations, when there is concern about heavy metals in the soil, dog faeces in the grass and microbes on every surface, your child's ability to explore his world can be limited. But it's vitally important that you devote time to fostering such early explorations and that you provide or find a safe, welcoming space where it can all happen at your child's pace. That may even mean becoming a full-time mum or dad for a while . . .

## Running free

Once, children ran free through fields, bushland or streets and on sand and grass. They climbed trees and scaled rock faces, scrambled over fences and walls and crawled through drainpipes. They built cubbyhouses and forts, rode bikes and billycarts. They played – fantasy, make-believe, creative stuff. And of course children still need to run free in wide-open spaces, to exercise all their muscles, to shout at the tops of their voices!

But today your child's leisure time may be full of structured activities and there's real concern about his safety if he roams unchecked and unsupervised. Since this structure and those safety concerns are facts of modern life, it's important that you take your child to a park, or to an oval or reserve as often as you possibly can. Let him run wild and you'll be surprised how much calmer he'll be.

Children of earlier generations also walked or cycled to and from school. Running, climbing, swimming and riding occupied them after school and on weekends and during holidays. Today children are invariably driven to school and to and from extracurricular activities. They may also spend a great many of their after-school hours in front of a computer screen or television set, or hunched over a desk or a musical instrument.

JAN ROBERTS

But your child doesn't need to become a couch potato or a slave to his hobbies or his studies. However, getting him off his backside and out of the house takes a conscious effort on your part, and that effort begins in his very earliest days. It also means that you have to set a good example.

## An overweight world?

A major concern for governments and public health delivery systems today is the number of overweight schoolchildren. Most of those overweight youngsters will grow to be overweight or even obese adults, who will inevitably suffer from a variety of weight-related health problems. Some experts claim that by the year 2050 just about everyone will be overweight, which means the rates of infertility and of chronic degenerative diseases such as hypertension, cardiovascular disease, diabetes and cancer – all of which have part of their origins in obesity – will reach epidemic proportions. It also means that the fit and well population won't be sufficient to take care of the numbers of unfit and unwell!

Don't let your child become part of this epidemic – get him moving now!

## 3. Exercise as a family

Do you wonder how you'll find the time or the energy to exercise? It might surprise you, but you'll actually find that you have more of both when you make exercise a regular part of your day.

The most important example that you can set is the one you set for your children. How can you expect them to enjoy Little Athletics when the nearest you've come to athleticism is watching men and women in lycra on your 42-inch plasma screen? So make this your movement mantra: the family that plays together stays together – and start exercising as a family. Expose your child to lots of different activities – you may even discover some new ones that you enjoy too!

127

Your own passion for physical activity can very easily include your child and can be adapted for his increasing levels of ability and strength. The physical activity doesn't have to be of the expensive kind, nor will your own passion necessarily become your child's. However, I am suggesting that exercise or regular physical activity of some description should become a normal part of your child's life and so much a part of his life that he continues well beyond school years, which is the time when many people completely lose the habit.

You might like to try some of the following . . .

## Jogging

If running is your thing, you can now buy sturdy, three-wheeled buggies that can accommodate one or two children. I told you there'd be a time for the chariot! Just remember what I said earlier about the disconnection between the jogger and joggee if your passenger is enclosed under a shade cloth and if you're plugged into your iPod or MP3 player. Make sure your passenger can see where he's going and that he's aware of your presence. Of course, with two sturdy youngsters as passengers and a commentary to be provided at the same time, you might prefer to swap that jog for a brisk walk.

## Cycling

If you're a committed cyclist, there are trailers for a passenger that can be towed behind your bike. Trailer bikes actually allow a child to pedal while still attached to the adult's bicycle. If your child is very young, or if he's happier when he's closest to you, a carrier behind or in front of your own seat may provide the answer. Just remember that your child must be able to sit by himself before he can ride in one of these devices, and if you're in the habit of taking extended rides, you'll need to choose a model that can recline, or that can support a sleepy head. Don't forget, too, that a helmet is an essential item for your bike-riding child.

## Bushwalking

Walking and hiking with your child is a wonderful way to encourage not only a comfortable attitude to exercise, but a love of the outdoors. Small legs can walk a surprisingly long way and your child will have a wonderful sense of achievement, even if you give him a helping hand by letting him finish the walk on your back. You can start with local walks in your area and work up to somewhere more adventurous as he gets older. Bushwalks offer a wide variety of experiences, including the opportunity to spot wildflowers and wildlife and perhaps even rock carvings or paintings.

## Water sports

If you're into boating, you'll need to invest in a life jacket of the appropriate dimensions for your child and also make sure your child is comfortable, both in and on the water, before you set sail. This is particularly important if there's any chance at all that your canoe or rowing boat might get swamped. Remember too that flapping sails and barked commands can frighten a small child, although if he's introduced to sailing or boating at an early age, he'll become very sure-footed.

You can also teach an extremely young child to swim – my boys had their first swimming lesson when they were just six weeks old and could swim unaided by the time they were two. Becoming water safe is as vitally important as becoming road safe, especially in warm countries such as Australia.

## Strength training

Committed to building muscle? I am, knowing all the benefits of increased muscle mass, as the years advance. But what about strength training for children? Research, reported in *Pediatrics*, November 2010, has shown that children and teenagers can increase their muscle strength with regular work-outs. Benefits include increased bone density and reduced body fat, with the kids' risk of injury no greater than for any other form of exercise or sport when training correctly and with supervision. The findings support the recommendations from the National Strength and Conditioning Association (NSCA) that children should do strength training two to three times a week under professional supervision. The local gym, youth or sporting club is a good place to begin these programs. Some aerobic and flexibility training should be incorporated too.

## 4. Yoga for kids

Another way to shape your child's attitude to movement and exercise, as well as to life in general, is to introduce him to yoga. All my earlier books outlined the benefits that yoga confers with regular practice – and children are no exception. Even if you've never practised yoga yourself, you can learn and enjoy the benefits at the same time.

If nothing else, yoga is wonderful for improving flexibility. A young child is naturally quite flexible, but as he gets older, and as more and more hours are spent at a desk or a computer, that natural tendency is lost. Being flexible means that muscles will be supple and ready for activity and movement. Increased flexibility also means reduced tension and stiffness and less likelihood that your child will sustain an injury when he plays sport or does other forms of exercise. Lots of elite athletes now include yoga in their training sessions for good reason.

Yoga can also increase strength and, of course, it's a great way to relax. The poses, or asanas, can help a child to be calm and focused and can also foster development of his concentration skills. Finally, yoga confers benefits if there are specific health issues such as coordination or learning problems, sleeping difficulties, headaches or constipation.

Visualisations can also be incorporated into the practice. This may well appeal to your child because he experiences so much of his emotional life through his body. Without any difficulty at all, his imagination will let him become a cobra, a bird, a dog or a tree. The various asanas don't need to be held as they do for adults, and your child can move through the sequences quite quickly. It's best not to perform any poses within two hours of eating, but apart from that, all you'll need is a mat or folded blanket, some loose, comfortable clothing and a book or DVD for beginners!

Here are a couple of simple asanas for you to try with your child.

## Tree pose

Start by shifting most of your weight to the left foot, making sure your inner foot stays firmly on the floor. This will be the tree trunk. Bend the right knee and as you do, reach down with your right hand, grasp the ankle and draw your foot up to rest on the inside of your left thigh. Toes should point down. Reach up, arms extended above your head with your palms facing inwards. Hold. Reverse. This is a good one for improving your child's balance.

## Downward-facing dog pose

Start with your hands and knees on the floor, with your hands under your shoulders. Spread your fingers apart. Your knees remain under your hips and slightly apart. Keep your spine straight and relaxed. Now breathe out and push your hips towards the ceiling, to form an inverted V. Back, legs and arms should stay straight – try to keep your heels on the floor. (Kids will love how one yoga teacher describes the correct posture for this asana: imagine you have a torch stuck in your bum and you need to shine the light on the ceiling!) Go from downward-facing dog to child's pose.

## Child's pose

Kneel with your knees together on the floor then sink back so that your buttocks touch your heels. Place your forehead on the ground and reach your arms straight out in front of you, palms turned down. You can vary this position by splaying your knees out to the sides – called extended child's pose. This position can be alternated with other asanas and you'll notice that your child will often adopt this one automatically when he's working or playing on the floor.

## Final relaxation pose

You can finish a session with some relaxation or meditation. Take your child through a guided visualisation in final relaxation pose. This is a wonderful opportunity to let your own (and his) imagination run riot – but just make sure all your images are bright and positive ones.

Lie on your back, keeping as still and symmetrical as you can. Close your eyes. Your hands should fall slightly away from your body and your palms should turn upwards. Let your feet fall slightly to the sides. Breathe slowly and steadily and feel your body getting heavy – relax into the ground. A visualisation or meditation, together with final relaxation pose, is a great way to get an unruly child to calm down, and can also be used in the evening to help him sleep.

## 5. Competitive sports

These days, a great deal of activity for children is very structured and is based around competitive team sports. But when it comes to competitive sports, there are some important considerations.

While I certainly recognise that working as a team, healthy competition and learning to be a good loser as well as a winner are important features of a child's social and personal growth, I deplore the attitude of many parents who live vicariously through their child's sporting successes and treat an under-tens soccer match as if it were the final of the FIFA World Cup! I also have grave doubts about the ability of a young child to understand that winning is not everything, particularly when he may struggle to distinguish in which direction his team's goalpost lies. When your child is really old enough to accept losing almost as graciously as he accepts winning, then he is ready for team sports.

Personally, I would prefer to see the whole family enjoy sport and leisure activities together and firmly believe that when children are young and impressionable, family-centred exercise activities are a better way to encourage a continuing commitment to regular exercise. But remember, whether it's a bushwalk or a canoe ride, whether it's a practice session or a grand final, it's your own attitude that will shape your child's. Make sure it's fun not fraught!

## 6. Travel with kids

'Harmony' and 'travelling with children' need not be mutually exclusive.

I have to admit that I'm hugely biased about the subject of travel with children. I think travel is simply one of the best, all-round educational experiences you can ever give a child and the memories are absolutely beyond price. I thank my own parents, who chose to spend money on holidays instead of on private schooling, for my love of travel and for a strong desire to give my boys the same experience. But a word of caution – travel is never without incident and is likely to be more so with children along for the ride, so some good advance planning is absolutely essential.

Part of your advance planning should involve a sure-fire way to settle a tired, overstimulated, bored, jet-lagged or otherwise fractious infant or toddler. It's one of the reasons why I strongly recommend extended breastfeeding – during all the trips we made when my boys were small, I was always able to calm, soothe, settle or simply nourish without any fuss or bother – which is, of course, quite an achievement if you've ever witnessed families on planes, buses and trains fruitlessly attempt to soothe a crying child. Some will rely on sedatives, which can sometimes have little or even the reverse effect, turning a journey into a nightmare for the family as well as for all those obliged to share the coach or the aircraft. If a sedative is what you're planning to use, be sure to give it a trial run ahead of time, remembering that the effect can sometimes vary from the one desired.

I suggest you stick close to home for your first forays into travel with kids. Remember that while you and your partner might still have the travel-lust and the urge to visit foreign parts, there are wonderful places to explore that are just an hour or two down the road. Your children won't know the difference when they're very young – everything is new and exciting to them.

Familiarity is another of my recommendations. This will make food selection and preparation easier, transport and accommodation choices less of a hassle and will also make dealing with the unexpected less problematic.

When choosing your destination, make sure it's somewhere that children are welcome and that there are lots of things for kids to do once you get there. With that in mind, you might be tempted to choose a resort where the kids are whisked away to be cared for by other people, but your children should also spend time with you too. Showing them the sights, joining in their activities, eating with them at mealtimes, watching them explore different cultures and deal with foreign languages down the track all provide innumerable opportunities for learning and also make for wonderful family memories.

I'm also a staunch advocate of trips by campervan. Every school holidays I embarked on family pilgrimages by campervan to beaches, forests, rivers and mountains. If you're tempted by the open road, my advice is to slow down, stop often, let the kids run around, and stretch their legs. It's important to make the journey just as interesting and as much fun as the destination.

To do so, you'll need to be sure to provide creative and fresh entertainment during the journey. Here are some ways to keep the kids from asking 'How much longer?' or 'When will we be there?'

- Singalongs – and that means everyone sings along!
- I-Spy
- Spotto
- Alphabet games
- Navigation games
- 'Wipe-clean' drawing devices
- And when all else fails . . . hand-held electronic games

There's no doubt that food can be used to get kids through what they perceive as the tedium of 'getting there' too. However, all of my recommendations for healthy eating habits apply stringently during car trips, which can prove a challenge when children can see chips, chocolates and fizzy drinks at every service station and roadside watering hole. Be warned – the short-term gains will be outweighed by longer-term feral behaviour in an enclosed space and ever-increasing demands for more of the same as the journey continues.

Advance planning is key. I suggest that before leaving home or setting off on the day's drive, you pack a few surprise treats that can be opened at opportune moments – these could include something that your child is not expecting or that he only enjoys infrequently, but make sure there's a limited supply if the treat is sweet.

The 'In your kitchen' section has lots of suggestions for healthy lunch boxes – and you can put them to good use on car trips. Remember, the protein portion will help to keep blood sugar levels from fluctuating. Don't forget several water bottles as well as wipes or moist towels for sticky fingers. A small hand-held vacuum cleaner can be used to great effect on car and campervan journeys.

So get out there and experience the world with your kids. I wish you lots of safe and happy journeys and many marvellous memories!

# THE MAGIC OF MOVEMENT:
# TEST YOUR KNOWLEDGE

Now you've learned about the importance of movement and exercise from a young age, you'll find some samples of the *flurishh* learning below. When you've answered the five multiple choice questions that follow, check your scores below. The correct answers to the 250 questions such as these will help you accrue points when you play the *flurishh* game at www.flurishh.com.

1. What's the best way to return to exercise after the birth of your baby?
1. Don't rush – traditionally women were secluded for eight weeks after birth
2. Get back to exercise quickly – it will restore energy levels
3. Make your baby part of your new exercise routine
4. Put your baby in a sling, focus on him, walk slowly and enjoy

2. When your mood, your energy levels, or your baby conspire against your exercise plan, what's your best option?
1. Do it anyway – it's vital for your and your baby's health
2. Do more than your normal routine – even if you hate every step
3. Skip it – but make up for it doubly tomorrow
4. Listen to your body, take a day off, relax, exercise tomorrow

3. Muscle is an organ, and muscle-building has important benefits that last a lifetime. Which of the following recommendations should you take if introducing older children or teenagers to strength training?
1. Professional supervision
2. Practise two to three times per week

3. Include aerobic and flexibility exercises too
4. All of the above

4. Babies from traditional societies are exposed to a constant range of movement. Which of the following activities are the most appropriate to accustom your child to an active life?
1. Massage and baby wearing
2. Team sports – from the sidelines
3. Exercise as a family, holiday in the outdoors
4. Team sports – on the field

5. Yoga has benefits for children as well as adults. What are they?
1. Improved posture and breath control
2. Improved circulation, delivery of oxygen and other nutrients
3. Improved ability to focus and stay calm
4. All of the above

**Answers**
**Q1:** 1. 2 pts, 2. 0 pts, 3. 2 pts, 4. 4 pts; **Q2:** 1. 0 pts, 2. 0 pts, 3. 0 pts, 4. 4 pts; **Q3:** 1. 1 pt, 2. 1 pt, 3. 2 pts, 4. 4 pts; **Q4:** 1. 2 pts, 2. 0 pts, 3. 2 pts, 4. 0 pts; **Q5:** 1. 2 pts, 2. 1 pt, 3. 1 pt, 4. 4 pts
(The maximum possible score is 20.)

# CHAPTER 6

## Be clean and green

### 1. Reduce toxicity

Did you know that the greatest chemical exposure occurs at home?

### 2. Avoid heavy metals

There are no safe levels of exposure to heavy metals for developing brains and bodies.

### 3. Vaccination

Look beyond the orthodox medical dogma and consider natural ways to enhance immunity.

### 4. Plastics

Plastics are incredibly useful and versatile, but they can have negative health effects. Here's what you need to know about them.

### 5. Radiation and mobile phones

There are two types of radiation – ionising and non-ionising, the latter now more commonly referred to as electromagnetic radiation – and both can have harmful effects on the body.

## 6. Children and TV and video/computer games

Put simply, watching TV and playing video or computer games reduces time available for other leisure activities.

## 7. Children and the cyberworld

In the space of less than a decade, the cyberworld with its chat rooms, online communities, social networks, massively multi-player games and all that these entail has become for many children, adolescents and even adults the source of friendships, relationships and for some individuals, their entire lives.

## 1. Reduce toxicity

Did you know that the greatest chemical exposure occurs at home?

You've done all you can to protect him in utero; now he's out in the real world. Your child will have to deal with unprecedented levels of environmental pollution during his lifetime and he is exquisitely sensitive to its effects while he's growing. The present-day chemical and heavy-metal cocktail has the potential for both short- and long-term effects, but your child's body also uses precious nutrients to detoxify these substances. Household cleaners, insect repellents, paint, the burn-off from an unflued gas heater, outgassing from carpet, furniture and timber, compounds in felt-tipped marker pens, glues and solvents used in model building, sunscreen and more all contribute to this cocktail. While some of them are inevitable, many can be avoided or replaced with non-toxic alternatives.

Providing a clean, green environment when your child is small is just as important for his health and wellbeing as it was for the health of the egg and sperm at conception and during his time in utero. Aim for natural fabrics, low-toxicity personal care products and an immediate environment free of chemicals, heavy metals and other toxins.

## Cotton nappies or disposables?

One of the first natural fabrics with which your baby will have contact is a cotton nappy. If you're appalled at the idea of soaking, washing and whitening old terry towelling squares and wrestling with nappy pins, rest assured that re-usable nappies have come a long way and are now shaped like disposables, include detachable cotton liners and may even contain a built-in waterproof outer liner. Nappy pins have also undergone a transformation!

Disposable nappies might seem a more desirable option, but consider the following facts.

- Many brands of disposables are potentially hazardous to babies. These extraordinarily absorbent, sweetly perfumed products – often colour-coded and complete with cute designs and graphics – may contain hazardous substances.

- Each year, 30 million trees are used in the manufacture of disposable nappies.

- Disposable nappies cause even greater environmental damage in landfill sites where the majority of them will remain for at least 200 years.

- Recently some researchers have suggested that disposable nappies lead to increased testicular temperature and may be responsible for declining sperm count, although the jury is still out on that one.

- Despite the claims of the manufacturers, there is absolutely no evidence that disposables reduce the incidence of nappy rash.

So if you're truly committed, you can protect your baby from potential toxic exposure, save yourself some money, and do the world's landfill sites a huge favour. Buy a supply of pure cotton nappies and wash them at 60°C (including a couple of times before their first use). Be sure to use an environmentally friendly soaker and laundry powder, or use baking soda and vinegar, and dry them in the sun. Alternatively, you might choose an eco-friendly nappy laundering service, but make sure they use softeners, washing powders and whiteners that are kind to your baby's skin and the environment.

Of course, this may sound like the worst kind of masochism. You could also argue that the chemicals, energy and water involved in laundering nappies are equally damaging to the environment. If you're going to use this line of argument to support your choice of disposables, you'll find a variety of 'green' disposable products that are free of dyes, fragrances and absorbing gels at your local organic shop or health food store. You might also find a brand that is completely biodegradable.

## Clothing and bedding

New clothing is also a potential source of chemical contamination. Much clothing contains traces of pesticides from crop spraying or to reduce pest damage while it's in storage, so always wash your baby's new clothes before he wears them. Flame-retardants, found in many pyjamas, are another potential hazard. You'll need to consider the likelihood of your child's exposure to an open fire or gas heater in making your choice.

Try to have natural fabrics in your baby's sleeping environment. This should include the materials used in the mattress, pillows (although your baby won't need one in his first two years) and bed linen. If he's sharing your bed, the same rules apply!

Look for organic cotton, bamboo, soy materials or merino wool. Hemp is also grown organically and all are better choices than synthetics.

## Personal care products

You might quite reasonably ask what earlier cultures used to keep their babies clean. They certainly didn't have the plethora of personal care products available to choose from today!

At birth the vernix that covers your baby's body is a wonderful moisturiser and shouldn't be washed off. If you can just leave his first bath for a few days, the vernix will be absorbed into his skin. The ancient Spartans used myrtle and wine in their infant's first bath and in medieval times soothing herbs such as chamomile, lavender or rose petals were added to the water. In the present day, the custom remains in most indigenous cultures.

There's no doubt that a lot of present-day personal care products are not only unnecessary but could be harmful. What's more, the smell of a new baby is incomparably wonderful! Why disguise it?

## Baby oil

Most commercial baby oils are actually light paraffin, which is a derivative of crude petroleum. Paraffin coats your baby's skin so that it cannot breathe and depletes his body of oil-soluble vitamins (such as vitamin D). By contrast, vegetable, nut and seed oils ensure that the vitamins remain in the body – try sweet almond, jojoba, olive or coconut. Store in dark glass and add the contents of a vitamin E capsule to the oil to prevent rancidity.

## Shampoo, soap, lotion

Many commercial products are brews of chemicals that include sodium lauryl sulphate and propylene glycol – both implicated in a variety of skin and eye problems. Castile soap (or a pure glycerin soap) is the best choice for your baby's bath and can also be used to wash his hair – put some apple cider vinegar in the rinsing water. Clean your baby's bottom with a moist face flannel and if you simply must dust him with powder, use cornflour instead of talcum.

## Toothpaste

Tooth brushing doesn't really become an issue until your child is eating meals with the family. Even then it's really not necessary to make a huge issue of it, given that those first teeth will be gone before too long. Still, it's an important habit to establish, but use natural toothpaste and avoid the ones containing fluoride. Alternatively, a new toothbrush developed in Japan has a light-sensitive titanium rod inside the handle – activated by light, it breaks down plaque but requires no paste.

## 2. Avoid heavy metals

There are no safe levels of exposure to heavy metals for developing brains and bodies.

Heavy metals are on the 'must-avoid' list at any time, from preconception through to breastfeeding. But the potential danger doesn't end there. Babies and young toddlers are particularly vulnerable. Toxic (heavy) metals can compromise your child's growth and brain development as they interfere with the body's enzyme systems.

The most widespread of the heavy metals is lead, and excessive ingestion during the years when your child's brain is developing can have severe effects. Lowered IQ levels caused by an even moderately elevated lead burden appear to be irreversible. Lead may be present in the soil close to roadways (a legacy of leaded petrol) and in backyards and parks in inner-city areas (legacies of leaded petrol, but also of previous industrial activity) – often in significant amounts. Old paint that has been scraped, sanded or burnt may deposit lead in the soil. Finally, old houses (especially those in inner-city areas) are a further source of lead-laden dust, and renovation will disturb this.

If your toddler plays in areas where lead is found, he's at risk because he engages in constant hand-to-mouth activity. As well, some children are not averse to eating dirt when they begin exploring their world and since lead compounds are sweet, this can lead to increased ingestion.

Cadmium, another heavy metal, has been implicated in behavioural and learning problems in young children. Since it is less widely distributed in the environment than lead, its adverse effects are less well publicised. Your child may build up significant levels of cadmium in his body if his diet includes a lot of products that contain sugar and refined flour, which are deficient in antagonistic trace elements. (Cadmium levels in the body will rise when levels of essential trace elements such as zinc are low.) Vegetables grown in cadmium-contaminated soils and shellfish found in estuaries close to industry are other potential sources. Cigarettes contain cadmium, which can be inhaled from passive smoke.

On the subject of cadmium in cigarette smoke, it's no secret that passive smoking can be very harmful. A child from the home of a smoker (or smokers) is more likely to suffer from respiratory ailments, compromised immunity and a number of other health problems such as middle ear infection, he is more likely to be a victim of SIDS, more likely to develop lung cancer and more likely to become a smoker himself – all compelling reasons for you or your partner to give up smoking and to keep your child away from passive smoke at all times. You'll find some helpful hints on kicking the habit in *Healthy Parents, Healthy Baby*.

Aluminium can lead to compromised nutritional status and has been linked with behavioural problems in children. It is found in cookware, aluminium foil and aluminium cans. Soy products may be high in aluminium and antiperspirants may be another source of exposure. Significant ingestion may occur if aluminium-containing products are used for infant reflux.

Limit your child's consumption of bottom-dwelling fish or fish that are high in the food chain, such as tuna and swordfish. Both may contain high levels of mercury. Another significant source of mercury ingestion by children is through thiomersal (called thimerosal in the US) which is a mercury-containing ingredient in vaccine products. Thanks to a great deal of adverse publicity surrounding its use, it has been replaced in many of the offenders. However, that doesn't mean that vaccines are safe on all counts – keep reading for natural ways to improve your child's immune competence.

## DID YOU KNOW?

It's been found that sidestream smoke is even more toxic than mainstream smoke itself.

## 3. Vaccination

Look beyond the orthodox medical dogma and consider natural ways to enhance immunity.

There's plenty of information around – both for and against childhood vaccination. You need to make your own decisions, but there's no doubt that the evidence is piling up against vaccination as the Holy Grail of keeping children free from infectious diseases.

This book is not the forum for a debate on the topic – despite the fact that I have very strong views. Having studied the orthodox dogma as well as the well-researched views opposing vaccination, I believe it is a procedure that exposes a very immature immune system to unnecessary and potentially damaging toxicity. It is also well known that the antigen-triggered antibody production which is the basis of vaccination comprises only a small part of the body's total immune response. Much more important, for example, is the health of the gut microbiota where 80 per cent of the body's immune response is mediated.

In making your decision, you should do your homework and find out about the potential side effects of childhood vaccination. The young Kennedy scion Robert Junior, standing in front of the House of Congress, speaking out against vaccination and describing the massive cover-ups of damning and incontrovertible evidence, is a good place to start your fact-finding mission. One of the most compelling articles I've read recently, 'The Danger of Excessive Vaccination During Brain Development' by Dr Russell Blaylock MD, explains the mechanism by which vaccine damage occurs. The Australian Vaccination Network (AVN) and the National Vaccine Information Center (NVIC) in the United States also provide a wealth of information about vaccines – all credible and fully researched.

### If you decide not to vaccinate . . .

If you choose not to vaccinate your child, you should be prepared to defend your choice, often in the face of large and powerful authorities such as education departments and hospitals. Arm yourself with the sorts of statistics that are available from sources such as the AVN and NVIC and know that vaccination is not compulsory in Australia! Nor is it true that the Child Allowance will not be paid for unvaccinated children.

If you decide to become a 'conscientious objector', I suggest you also find a medical practitioner or other health professional who'll support you and can offer orthodox or natural therapies if they're ever necessary.

## If you decide to vaccinate . . .

If, after considering the arguments for and against vaccination, you decide to vaccinate your child, then you should also consider the options that are available to reduce the possibility of side effects.

- Delay the start of the vaccination schedule – until his brain and immune system are more fully mature is a good place to start.
- If you prolong breastfeeding, your child will receive antibodies for as long as you continue to nurse him.
- Initially your child's immune system should be strong. If you've been following my Healthy Parents, Healthy Baby Program from before conception, you can be pretty sure you've given him immune competence.
- You can strengthen his immune system further with judicial use of nutritional supplements and high potency probiotics that contain human strains of bacteria.
- No vaccination should ever be given if your child is even mildly unwell, if he is teething or is under any other sort of stress.
- Isolation of the separate immune-stimulating elements will reduce the load on his system (e.g., triple antigen could be given

as three separate shots – diphtheria, tetanus, pertussis). Don't let your doctor say it can't be done – it can! While this approach increases the stress of the doctor's visit, it substantially reduces the amount of antigenic material that is injected at one time.

- Another option is to give only that which goes via normal channels, that is, by mouth, which allows your child's body to deal with the foreign protein in the normal way. The disadvantage of this method is that only polio vaccine is available as an oral dose, although some inhaled vaccines are being developed.
- Many natural therapists offer homoeopathic immunisation. Do your homework on the efficacy of this method too.
- Exercise particular caution if there's a history of allergy in your family or if children of family members had adverse responses to vaccines.

In summary I believe, as do all practitioners of natural and holistic medicine, that a strong and robust immune system is what your child really needs. As a matter of personal interest, I wasn't vaccinated as a child. This was a very radical stance taken by my mother at a time when polio was still seen as a serious threat. I had chicken pox, whooping cough, mumps and measles as a kid and got over them. Apart from the odd cold and flu, I've never been sick – in fact, I couldn't tell you when I last saw a doctor. I have never been to hospital – and both of my boys were born at home. Neither of them was vaccinated as a child. Dave has never seen a doctor, Mike only for an altercation with the bottom of the swimming pool. However, he was required to have several vaccinations as a student enrolling in a Nursing degree. As he was a very robust young man of 18, I had to accept that the potential for damage was infinitely less than for a two-month-old baby whose brain and immune systems are both still in highly vulnerable, developing stages!

Good luck in your fact-finding and your ultimate decision. I know what an enormously emotive issue this can be!

## DID YOU KNOW?

The developed nations with the most intensive vaccine program for their young have the highest infant mortality rate. A child born in the USA, subjected to 26 vaccinations, has the worst chance (comparing all developed nations) of reaching his first birthday.

## 4. Plastics

Plastics are incredibly useful and versatile, but they can have negative health effects. Here's what you need to know about them.

For many years, debate raged about the safety or otherwise of the widely used chemical product Bisphenol A, or BPA. Known since the 1930s to be oestrogenic (mimicking the effects of the female hormone), annual production of BPA is between 2–3 million tonnes, destined mostly for use in plastics, particularly food and drink containers. BPA leaches when heated. It was officially stated that there was no threat from small doses, but there is now incontrovertible evidence linking BPA to breast cancer, sex hormone imbalances, obesity and other serious health issues – as well as adverse health risks for foetuses, babies and young children. In 2009 baby bottle manufacturers in the USA removed BPA from their products. The following year European scientists began a campaign to lobby their governments to remove baby bottles containing BPA from shelves with the result that the European Union banned the use of Bisphenol A (BPA) in plastic baby bottles from 2011. You can act now to get this toxic substance out of your life.

Phthalates are another class of chemical added to plastics to make them soft and pliable – but which have been shown to have harmful health consequences. (They are also found in lotions and shampoos.) Like BPA, phthalates are hormone disruptors and have been linked to liver, kidney and testicular cancer.

For the guidelines on what the number inside the recycling symbol on various plastic products means, refer to *Healthy Parents, Healthy Baby* Chapter 7: Surrounds. Also remember this helpful mnemonic: '4 5 1 and 2 – all the rest are bad 4U' (Annie Murphy Paul, *Origins: How the Nine Months Before Birth Shape the Rest of Our Lives*).

## Toys

There's no doubt that wooden toys are preferable to plastic ones, but look for ones that are made with non-toxic glues, paints and varnishes. Rudolf Steiner's educational philosophy includes only wooden toys and both the Steiner and Montessori systems emphasise the choice of toys that are meaningful for the child. The numerous Montessori-based educational toys that are now available certainly have great and enduring value for a child – many of them being based in 'practical life'. Think about what your child prefers to play with – the things that he sees you use every day! Having said that, I don't know what my boys would have done without Lego, but equally a great many plastic toys are cheap, useless, completely meaningless to a child, easily broken and potentially toxic.

Choose carefully and thoughtfully – but good luck in getting gift-givers to do the same.

## 5. Radiation and mobile phones

There are two types of radiation – ionising and non-ionising, the latter now more commonly referred to as electromagnetic radiation – and both can have harmful effects on the body.

# Ionising radiation

Ionising radiation is particularly damaging to rapidly growing cells, with children and adolescents therefore especially vulnerable.

Most medical professionals are aware of the need to ensure that X-rays are only ordered when absolutely necessary. But professionals haven't always erred on the side of caution where X-rays are concerned. Back in the 1930s, X-rays were used routinely on pregnant women with a standard textbook on antenatal care stating confidently that there was no danger to the developing child if the procedure was carried out by a competent radiographer. A later edition of the same textbook stated: 'It is now known that the unrestricted use of X-rays through the fetus caused childhood cancer.'

Nowadays a visit to the dentist could still result in your child being exposed to a large dose of completely unnecessary radiation. The use of highly sophisticated and ever more powerful scanning devices, some even providing 3-D images, to give dentists precise information previously unavailable to them, reminds me of the indiscriminate use of X-rays in days gone by. Be aware of the potential for a dentist to use this new technology routinely – barely stopping to check whether you even want it.

# Electromagnetic radiation

These days it's almost impossible to avoid being exposed to electromagnetic radiation, or EMR, which has much more subtle impacts than ionising radiation. Long-term effects of exposure to this environmental pollutant are unknown but migraines and epileptic type fits in some children who spend hours in front of video games have been reported. However, these effects are really only part of the issue.

Electromagnetic radiation is entirely unseen – therefore insidious – and certain to become more problematic as time goes on, especially when you consider that exposure (thanks largely to mobile phone technology and wireless networks and hot spots) is many million times what it was just 20 years ago.

Your child will experience previously unimaginable levels of EMR exposure from mobile phones because their use now begins at a very early age. After all, when he sees you talking on your mobile up to a dozen times a day, it should be no surprise that he wants to play with yours and soon wants one of his own. There is, of course, a strong argument for providing your school-aged child with a phone to stay in touch with parents or make contact in an emergency; however, this easy contact comes with a significant downside – the risks of exposure to EMR.

In fact, many experts perceive the explosion of mobile phone use as a large-scale health disaster in the making, contributing to a potential epidemic of neurological issues – particularly for children, whose developing nervous systems and thinner skulls make them extremely vulnerable to damage from electromagnetic radiation. Significantly, in February 2011 the *Journal of the American Medical Association* published the results of the first and largest study to clearly show that the weak radio-frequency signals from mobile phones have the potential to alter brain activity.

A number of scientists and government agencies in Europe have also accepted that EMR from mobile phones does pose health risks, with some countries orchestrating public health campaigns designed to warn schoolchildren of the dangers of mobile phones, posting notices in schools and community halls. The Vienna Medical Association called for a ban on mobile phone advertising targeting children and adolescents. Erik Huber, environment advisor for the association, has stated: 'Children under the age of 16 should never use a mobile phone. Scientists do not argue anymore whether mobile phones are harmful, but rather how harmful they are.'

The US Environmental Working Group offers the following helpful tips in reducing your and your child's exposure to mobile phone radiation.

1. Buy a low-radiation phone. [Check the charts that compare phones.]
2. Use a headset or speaker.
3. Listen more, talk less. [More radiation is emitted when you're broadcasting.]
4. Hold the phone away from your body.
5. Choose texting over talking when possible. [Less radiation is emitted when sending SMS and importantly, when texting, the phone is kept away from your head.]
6. Poor signal? Stay off the phone. [More radiation is emitted in low signal areas.]
7. Limit children's phone use. [Children's brains absorb twice the amount of mobile phone radiation as an adult's.]
8. Skip the 'radiation shield'. [Phone covers and antenna caps force the phone to transmit more radiation.]

To those tips, I would add the following . . .

- Don't use your mobile when wearing or nursing your baby.
- Keep out of pockets – away from your reproductive organs. Do not attach to your belt either.
- If you have nowhere else to put it and must carry your phone on your person, switch it to 'flight' mode.

## Wi-fi

Blake Levitt, author of *Electromagnetic Fields: A Consumer's Guide to the Issues and How to Protect Ourselves*, states it simply. 'All of these concerns [electromagnetic radiation from mobile phones and transmitter towers] . . . also apply to the Wi-Fi networks in our homes and libraries and offices and cafés and parks and neighborhoods.' Levitt considers it ironical that residents will demonstrate against the erection of a transmitter tower in their neighbourhood, yet they will install wireless networks in their homes and offices. The 'pollution' caused by these networks, which have sprung up all over the world, appears to be taken much more seriously in Europe than elsewhere, with a number of initiatives worthy of note.

In early 2008, the National Library of France shut down its wi-fi system, citing possible 'genotoxic effects'. Hot on the heels of the National Library's action, the staff at the Library Sainte-Geneviève, also in Paris, filed a petition demanding that wi-fi be replaced with wired connections. Several European governments are moving to prohibit wireless networks in government buildings and educational institutions, while the Austrian Medical Association is pushing for a ban on wi-fi systems in schools, pointing to the danger to children in particular.

A while ago, I read a disturbing article in *The New York Times* ('The Pacifier Gets an Upgrade: Apps and Gadgets to Soothe the Baby', 24 November 2010) written by a new father, Farhad Manjoo, who was totally seduced by the various apps and gadgets that he could use to pacify his son. While his baby was still in hospital, he decided his newborn needed help getting to sleep, so for just $1.99 he downloaded an app called 'White Noise' and, after putting his phone a few centimetres from his son's ear, soon saw him drift off to sleep. The article made me wonder how close to the truth for many parents Manjoo's statement, 'My house is a menagerie of motorized baby seats, noisemakers, monitors and other doodads that promise to bring digital sophistication to a job that has reduced adults to tears forever', was. He described a digital camera which beamed video of his baby across the world so he could check in with his son at any time, apps to help decode his baby's cries and remind him to feed, change and rest his baby, and a sensor pad that was placed under the mattress, which warned him if his baby hadn't moved for 20 seconds. But his favourite device was one that lit up and played soothing 'womb sounds' when the baby cried in the middle of the night! Talk about devices designed to foster discon-nection between parents and babies! In my mind, this substitution of electronic gadgetry for human touch and presence is probably the greater and the sadder issue, but also, please give your baby a break from electromagnetic pollution in his most immediate environment for as long as you possibly can. His inevitable exposure to EMR will happen soon enough . . .

## 6. Children and TV and video/computer games

Put simply, watching TV and playing video or computer games reduces time available for other leisure activities.

Most children today spend countless hours in front of television and computer screens. You can try to rationalise it, claiming that some computer games and television programs are educational and that regardless, children need to be able to use these tools if they are to make their way in the modern world. But the reality is these electronic babysitters don't offer the stimulation and the learning and develop-mental experiences that are provided when children are engaged in conversation, storytelling and in simple outdoor or play activities.

At a time when a child should be learning to use his imagination, to conjure up all sorts of images from within, the electronic media bombards him with a multitude of ready-made images. He does not need to respond in any way to what he sees and hears. If your child watches television for several hours each day on a daily basis during his early years, he has really learned nothing. In fact, his developing brain has received no more benefit than if he had watched the same program countless times. (On the contrary, when you watch television you bring to your viewing a lifetime of experience and knowledge and you also have the ability to be critical, discerning and selective . . . well, I'll give you the benefit of the doubt.)

By the time the average child has finished high school he will have spent more hours watching television than he has spent at school.

By the time he is 70 he will have spent seven years watching TV. He will have seen countless acts of violence, murder and explicit sex, not to mention umpteen advertisements for foods that are high in fat, sugar, salt and added chemicals. Numerous studies have looked at the effects of TV viewing on children, with varying conclusions drawn, but there seems to be universal agreement that TV makes children more aggressive, harms their acquisition of reading skills, decreases their creativity test scores and cuts their non-TV leisure activities.

A study, published in *Pediatrics*, November 2010, found that more than two hours a day spent watching television or playing video or computer games is linked to emotional or behavioural problems in children. Significantly, it showed that these psychological problems held, no matter how much time was spent doing physical activity to 'compensate' for time spent in front of the box. 'It wasn't clear whether having high physical activity levels would "compensate" for high levels of screen viewing in children,' study co-author Angie Page, a professor at the University of Bristol in England, was reported as saying in an article published in *Live Science*, 'Exercise Doesn't Make Up for Kids' Screen Time', 11 October 2010. 'It seems more like what you are doing in that sedentary time that is important, i.e., if you choose to spend large number of hours screen viewing for entertainment, then this is associated with negative mental well-being.'

There are several ways in which you can respond to the TV and electronic game dilemma. But you should always remember – and it's a potent mantra for your parenting stances in general – you are in charge!

You can ban electronic media completely, which will give your child the best opportunity to become self-motivated and to play creatively. He may even become a keen reader. However, he may also feel very left out when peers discuss television programs or video games and may even resist bringing friends home because he's self-conscious about the lack of TV, Wii or PlayStation, or become resentful. Also the whole family might miss out on worthwhile educational programs.

You can limit his viewing or playing time. Theoretically this is a very attractive option – but for busy parents it can become a nightmare of trying to ensure that limited viewing time is restricted to quality programs and of trying to avoid constant pleadings of 'just one more program' or 'just till the end of the show'.

You can confine the TV to a special room that does not impinge on the family lifestyle. This is an attractive option if you watch no TV yourself, but it also means that you may be unaware of what programs your child is in fact watching or what games he's playing.

Of course, TV and video and computer games seem relatively simple issues when I think about what future parents might be facing. Still, my best advice to you is to take charge and set a good example. If you have a full, busy life that involves little TV and all other electronic gadgetry in moderation, and if your child sees you reading books, listening to or playing music, pursuing hobbies, working in the garden, or otherwise engaged in a variety of activities, hopefully he'll follow suit.

On the subject of reading, of course electronic book readers provide a whole new reading dimension – one that your digital-native will probably embrace with enthusiasm. I confess I'm addicted to my Kindle – taking it with me everywhere I go and consequently reading three times more books than before. The interesting fact about the burgeoning ebook market is that it does not appear at this stage to be cannibalising the real book market – with many readers buying both, a whole new market of ebook readers is emerging! And this emerging market could include your child.

With regard to potential radiation, a device such as the Kindle uses 'electronic ink', so when reading books, newspapers or magazines that are already stored on the device, electric current is used, with little resulting radiation. Just remember to keep your reader well away from your body and switch the wireless connection off when the download (which usually takes less than 60 seconds) is complete. Ebooks can also be read on PCs, laptops and iPads – no doubt other options are just around the corner. Of course, you'll need to do your research on the best protective devices, eyestrain, downloading undesirable reading material, and possible addiction to such devices.

## 7. Children and the cyberworld

In the space of less than a decade, the cyberworld with its chat rooms, online communities, social networks, massively multi-player games and all that these entail has become for many children, adolescents and even adults the source of friendships, relationships and for some individuals, their entire lives. In 2011, 'World of Warcraft', often referred to as 'WoW', which is a Massively Multiplayer Online Role-Playing Game (MMORPG), currently the world's most subscribed MMORPG, surpassed 10 million subscribers worldwide. The casual gaming space is an equal if not more startling phenomenon – with the Zynga development 'Farmville', played on Facebook, in 2010 counting more than 80 million players, 25 million of whom were said to play on a daily basis!

I'm far from immune to the power of these new media, having leapt into the interactive space with my own *flurishh* game.

In fact, it was my younger son Mike's passion for online games that encouraged me to look more closely at this phenomenon and recognise that there certainly are opportunities for learning and working within a collaborative community, and that they could even be a family affair (particularly in the case of MMORPG) and that it wasn't all doom and gloom. But more importantly I listened to what Mike said about his passion, asked questions, watched him at play and tried to understand. I trust that my game and many like it will use this new engaging and entertaining medium for good and positive things. I am hugely excited about the opportunity that this presents – to take this new generation of game-players and translate their mindset into positive action in the real as opposed to the virtual world.

Of a different genre, but equally ubiquitous in their reach and influence, are social networks such as Facebook, MySpace, Twitter and many more. These are here to stay, they will undoubtedly evolve into other communication channels and the influences are certainly not all negative; it's just vital that a child learns how to integrate them appropriately into the wider context of his life.

With no guidance given or balance shown, video and computer games give your child the opportunity to be a virtual participant in violence and mayhem while online communities open him to being bullied or groomed or to bully others in a very real way. The additional issue of posting thoughtless, hurtful or deeply personal and inappropriate images, videos or messages that are out there for the whole world to see or read – and which may appear for years to come – is heady stuff, with even the potential to change lives. Educating your child about how to conduct himself in the online world should begin early and be an ongoing process.

I realise, of course, that many of you who are reading will be totally immersed in this online world yourselves. However, an amazing transformation can take place when you become a parent – you want only the very best for your child. You may very well decide that you'd like your child to spend less time than you do surfing, posting, tweeting, role-playing or being otherwise connected to other worlds. Once again, remember that encouraging your child to do as you do is going to be infinitely more effective than to do as you say! It's the example you set when they're very small that will hopefully give them some sort of balance when they're old enough to make their own choices.

So my advice – know the pitfalls of electronic gadgetry and the access that it can provide to inappropriate worlds. Moderate its use wherever you can, especially when it is completely within your control. Don't be afraid to take this step! However, remain present, interested and communicative, if and when it assumes more significance in your child's life than you consider fair and reasonable. I guess this all comes back to the importance of trusting your child, trusting your parenting, but also acknowledging that there is a whole world out there which no doubt will continue to confound and confuse parents. The challenge is to remain tolerant and tactful – no child will ever have a real relationship with, or take advice from, someone who is a constant critic.

# BE CLEAN AND GREEN:
# TEST YOUR KNOWLEDGE

Now you've learned all about how to provide a healthy and safe home environment for children, you'll find some samples of the *flurishh* learning below. When you've answered the five multiple choice questions that follow, check your scores below. The correct answers to the 250 questions such as these will help you accrue points when you play the *flurishh* game at www.flurishh.com.

1. When you close your front door on the world, your exposure to environmental pollution actually increases. Do you know where it comes from?
1. Personal care and household cleaning products
2. Products in kitchen, bathroom, laundry, garage and workshop
3. Timbers, paints, furnishings, carpet
4. Toxicity off the soles of shoes into the carpets and onto floors

2. The ubiquitous plastic packaging has been linked to hormone disruption and other problems. What can you do to limit your exposure to harmful plastics?
1. Avoid all packaging unless absolutely necessary
2. Choose glass, cardboard or paper containers
3. Choose plastics with 4, 5, 1 and 2 in the recycling symbol
4. Put all plastic packaging in the recycling bin

3. Cadmium is a heavy metal that causes serious health issues, especially in children. Which of the following are

potential sources of cadmium? Score 1 for each correct answer

1. Cigarette smoke (passive or active)
2. Shellfish
3. Refined flour products
4. Sugar-containing products

4. Do you know how much of the energy will be absorbed into your head while you're on a mobile phone call?

1. 30 per cent
2. 70 per cent
3. 50 per cent
4. 20 per cent

5. How can you reduce the potential health issues associated with mobile phones?

1. Buy a low-radiation phone
2. Use a headset or speaker
3. Keep the phone at least 30 cm away from any body part
4. All of the above and no mobiles for my children

**Answers**

Q1: 1. 3 pts, 2. 4 pts, 3. 3 pts, 4. 1 pt; Q2: 1. 4 pts, 2. 3 pts, 3. 3 pts, 4. 1 pt; Q3: 1. 1 pt, 2. 1 pt, 3. 1 pt, 4. 1 pt; Q4: 1. 0 pts, 2. 4 pts, 3. 0 pts, 4. 0 pts; Q5: 1. 2 pts, 2. 2 pts, 3. 2 pts, 4. 4 pts

(The maximum possible score is 20.)

# CHAPTER 7

## Mothers matter too

### 1. Choose happiness
Some individuals have a personality blueprint that is better geared for happiness, yet we all have the potential to shape our experiences.

### 2. Nurture your baby and yourself
Value your mothering role and remember, no one else can do it quite like you.

### 3. What about child care?
Think homebirth and childhood vaccination are emotive topics? Well, the topic of child care is right up there among them.

### 4. Are you planning another baby?
If this book is your first introduction to the Healthy Parents, Healthy Baby Program and you want to prepare for another pregnancy, the following summary gives you the lowdown.

# 1. Choose happiness

Some individuals have a personality blueprint that is better geared for happiness, yet we all have the potential to shape our experiences.

The emerging field of epigenetics confirms that the memory of emotional experiences of past generations is carried in our DNA, so to some extent we are hard-wired for a basic level of happiness or unhappiness. In accepting that, I also believe that we can all live more fulfilled lives and at each moment in our lives we can actively choose to be happy.

To do so, we need to let go of past hurts and grievances, to live in the moment without judgement and also to recognise that life is not designed to be an endless pleasure cruise. As a parent, in particular, you will experience both challenges and triumphs, disappointment and achievement. But if there were no lows, you would not enjoy the elation of the highs; if you never knew failure, you wouldn't learn how to go forward to succeed. *Care of the Soul: A Guide for Cultivating Depth and Sacredness in Everyday Life*, by Thomas Moore, is a book I love for its wisdom and erudition, but also for its clear statement in favour of willing acceptance of the moments when happiness is elusive.

My life's work has revolved around producing a healthier, happier next generation. While the optimal physical health of prospective parents – that is to say, prior to conception – is a prerequisite for the optimal physical health of their children, I also believe that optimal emotional health established in early infancy can lay very firm foundations for happiness in later life. At the very least, those firm foundations are the best insurance for when things get tough, or when the genetic blueprint conspires against the attainment of happiness.

Establishing optimal emotional health in infancy requires some very committed parenting practices – and sadly, these are practices that are in danger of becoming extinct. In my view, if you are to establish the groundwork for an emotionally healthy adult, one who will have the greatest potential for choosing happiness over unhappiness, start very early! Attending to your baby's every cry is a great starting point. Becoming a baby-wearing and co-sleeping mum or dad is another. Knowing that the work you are doing as a parent is the most important and fulfilling job you will ever undertake is yet another.

But if you're really committed to fostering a happier next generation, you need to care for yourself too.

## 2. Nurture your baby and yourself

Value your mothering role and remember, no one else can do it quite like you.

While your baby's tiny, your role in providing appropriate food, drink and safe, clean surroundings is a given. But you can provide other things too, such as a comforting, stimulating environment, that are equally important for his growth and development. Though these are entirely focused on your baby, they have a positive spin-off effect on your own mental and emotional wellbeing and they are not just about now, they last into the future. Nature is extraordinarily clever and when your baby gets what's best for him, there are huge benefits for you as well.

Make the most of the time when your baby can be carried in your arms. Those months are incredibly short, even though it sometimes doesn't feel that way. In a very short space of time your baby will learn an amazing amount. Every new movement, sight, sound, texture, colour and, later, taste and flavour are the raw materials that his highly absorbent brain demands. Provide them!

In earlier times (and still in some cultures today) a baby went everywhere with his mum. If she was unavailable, a close family member would take over, but that baby was always carried close. He saw all the goings-on of his large extended family, was an integral part of their day-to-day food-gathering and preparation, their household chores, their journeys and migrations, their rituals and celebrations. He heard their conversations, their music and their stories. All of this occurred without conscious thought or effort on anyone's part.

However, lifestyles and communities have changed dramatically and today's nuclear family provides a totally different environment. Unfortunately, biology hasn't kept pace with those profound changes. Your baby's early development still occurs to best advantage when he's exposed to constant movement and a massive number and constant variety of stimuli. That stimulation will be most efficiently processed when your baby's in a place of absolute safety and security. Now it's up to you to create that truly stimulating environment that once was his as a matter of course.

This means taking your baby with you wherever you go and exposing him to all the sights and sounds of your day. This may not be as quick or convenient as leaving him at home, but remember that even getting ready and organised is part of his learning process. Remember too that what you're doing actually has incalculable benefits for his cognitive development. Carrying him in a sling or snuggly makes getting around with him far easier than using a pram or stroller. It also leaves both hands free for chores and other children. Take him shopping, to meetings, to a lunch with your girlfriends or for your walk.

Your baby will enjoy your constant conversation. That doesn't mean baby talk. That means normal running commentary on things that interest you and capture your attention. Don't contrive it – make it real stuff that you would say to any other companion. If you're the quiet type, or if you feel slightly ridiculous carrying on a conversation with a tiny baby, pointing out things that he can't actually recognise yet, just remind yourself that his brain is capable of absorbing a massive amount of information. The more information you put in, the more that brain absorbs and the more you talk to him, the sooner he'll begin to understand and respond.

The more conversations you have, even though they're one-sided, the more in tune you become with his own method of communication, however rudimentary that might be. Before he becomes articulate, you'll learn to distinguish his needs from a range of cries, gurgles and shouts. The more adept you become at deciphering what your baby wants and the quicker you respond, the better he feels about himself. But this isn't a one-way street – your reward comes through improved feelings about your ability as a mother. How many new mums have you seen depicted as totally puzzled by a screaming baby? 'What do you want?' is their constant refrain.

When your baby's old enough you can initiate games and activities. The more time you spend showing and helping, the more intimate your knowledge of his ability and his particular interests. Being very aware of his limitations and capabilities, you'll offer him jobs that he can master, and the greater his ability to cope with and manipulate his environment successfully, the higher his self-esteem will be. 'Let me do it myself!' is the young child's catchcry.

This positive feedback loop – dare I say it – works to best advantage with a full-time mum interacting with her own child. As you get better at your job, you'll find that your toddler's demands take less effort and become more of a pleasure than a trial. As he becomes better at initiating and continuing this subtle interaction, so his demands become less constant. Along with this wonderful interplay, your own self-esteem increases and you send positive signals about your child's self-worth back to him.

If this dynamic sounds very idealistic, remember that the hormones prolactin and oxytocin facilitate this interaction. I've already told you all about the benefits of oxytocin – the 'love' drug, the hormone of calm and connection. When you breastfeed, you and your baby are awash in it. (Keep in mind that the benefits continue into the future, too. The longer you breastfeed, the less likely you are to experience challenging symptoms at menopause.) Prolactin, the 'mothering' hormone, is also secreted during breastfeeding. Its extraordinary properties make you more patient, relaxed, intuitive and as a result better able to cope with your baby's needs.

Much-reduced or zero levels of oxytocin and prolactin – the result of complementary feeds, early introduction of solids or weaning – lead to a vicious cycle. The less of these hormones you have, the less patience you have with your baby. The less patience you have, the harder it is for you to fill all his needs. The more difficult you find things, the less intuitively you will respond and the more likely you are to put him on a bottle, give him solids, let him cry at night and the more appealing returning to work becomes. So the downhill slide gathers momentum. The marvellous scheme that has served women and their babies well for countless generations is disrupted with incalculable losses for all concerned.

In the early months with a new baby, it's very easy to become focused solely on his needs to the exclusion of your own, especially neglecting practical things such as eating well and exercising regularly. Looking after your physical self is just as important as it ever was, and there's also the very real possibility that before too long, you'll want to have another baby. (Don't misunderstand me – I'm not suggesting you have another before your older one is reasonably independent!) You'll want to be in the best possible shape when you conceive again, so don't forget the importance of excellent preconception health care second or third time around.

Making sure that your child gets the very best of you means taking a close look at what's really important. What about all those jobs you're trying to do? You might be expected to be wife, mother, lover, housekeeper, taxi-driver, community activist, breadwinner and maybe even careerwoman as well. Nature never intended you to be so many things to so many people! As a modern mum you not only expect much more of yourself, but do much more than a woman of an earlier generation. As well, your support groups of close-knit community and the extended family of an earlier age are gone. During those early months, especially while you're breastfeeding, make nurturing yourself and your child your most important priority. Don't try to keep your house in the same immaculate condition as in your childless days; forget the dust and the cobwebs for a while. Give up the gourmet meals and entertaining and, if late nights exhaust you, put your social life on the backburner too. The same advice applies to all your other roles as well. Most importantly, when your baby has a sleep, lie down with him – don't waste his nap time doing all the jobs around the house.

Today, the mum who stays at home to care for a young family is an anomaly – a quick return to work after her baby's birth is often worn as some sort of high-achievement award. If you've worked your way up the career ladder, the months or years that you take off to raise your children may loom as an obstacle to promotion and future success. It's a pity that many women see this time as one of complete hiatus in their lives. It's also a sad reflection on the values of contemporary society that the bearing and raising of children is not perceived as a career that is every bit as rewarding and fulfilling as those more generally associated with the word. On a positive note, in Australia we've recently seen the introduction of some more enlightened government regulations covering maternity and paternity leave. I sincerely hope these will make full-time mothering and fathering a much more viable option for many families. Other countries, such as Sweden and Norway which have some of the most generous maternity leave in the world, certainly recognise that at least one full-time parent during the child's early years pays massive long-term dividends.

While you may not miss the climb up the corporate ladder, you may miss the financial rewards of full- or part-time work. If you aspire to having a bigger home for your growing family, which drives your plan to return to work, remember that a small child does not really need his own space. He needs to be close to parents and brothers and sisters. He will happily play at your feet, sleep in your bed and generally share your life for a long time before he feels the need to be separate. If you give him the chance to do so, if you don't consign him to his own sterile spaces, he'll be a much happier child.

If you're working to pay for his education, remember that the best foundations are laid at home. Today, many parents see child-raising as a bid for the best and brightest opportunities (not to mention the best and brightest child). Their focus becomes not just the right school, but lessons in music, swimming, dancing or drama with extracurricular training for soccer, cricket, football and more. This isn't to say that all these skills and accomplishments have no value – indeed, introducing your child to educational excellence and a host of different activities is a wonderful thing. But it's not the Holy Grail!

More than anything else, your child needs your commitment and time during his early years. The closeness and togetherness that you give him now is the best and surest way to foster a well-adjusted, happy, caring and responsible teenager and adult. If your child has your time, then the school that he attends can only build on the groundwork that you've already laid. If you haven't been there to lay this groundwork, no amount of expensive schooling, lessons or tuition, not to mention material goods, can make up for what your child has missed. So be there – fully – for these precious years!

## 3. What about child care?

Think homebirth and childhood vaccination are emotive topics? Well, the topic of child care is right up there among them. It has its detractors, such as well-known parenting author Steve Biddulph, who says that child care 'used "too much, too early, too long" damages babies' brain chemistry and affects their social and emotional development'. And it has its proponents, committed to the provision of 'quality child care' to help women achieve equality and make their mark in the public and private sector.

Now, don't get me wrong – I'm all for women gaining whatever ground they can in whatever way they can. If we had more women in the workplaces and the governments of the world, the world would be a very different and a far better place – of that I'm absolutely certain. But I also believe that can still happen and women can also have the opportunity to be full-time mums – because babies really flourish with a consistent full-time caregiver in those early years.

I first heard Steve Biddulph speak at a homebirth conference not long after my son David was born and Biddulph's passion and commitment to the raising of truly happy, healthy families has never diminished. Thirty-five years in the business, and 4 million book sales to his credit, he makes no bones about the international body of developmental and neurobiological research, which clearly shows 'that at least during the first two years of life, brain development unfolds at its optimum with one-to-one care'.

Interestingly, Biddulph hasn't always been an advocate of full-time mothering (or fathering), but completely reversed his previous belief in quality day care during five years spent researching his book *Raising Babies: Should under 3s go to nursery?* One of the most telling, of many significant findings, is the higher cortisol levels observed in children in long day care. Cortisol, one of the stress hormones, is linked to anxiety and to more aggressive behaviour, but is also known to affect the development of a range of neurotransmitters and brain pathways that are still being formed. These altered brain patterns in babies and young children are long-lasting, adversely affecting the way these children respond to stress and anxiety in later life.

Biddulph believes that the corporatisation of child care has made child-raising something of a conveyor belt affair, with children in centres cared for 'in bulk'. He believes that as a vast social experiment, the results are now emerging and they are not favourable – with a worldwide epidemic of teenage depression, anxiety and substance abuse.

I believe that Biddulph's comments add weight to the intuitive anxiety that many women (and their partners) experience on placing their child in day care. However, I don't want to add to the feelings of guilt that parents often feel in equal measure. Rather, I hope that you might reassess where your role as a mother (in particular) stands in the bigger context of your life.

Mothering has fallen from favour as something of fundamental importance and great intrinsic value, so use the gifts that Nature has bestowed on you. There'll be time again for 'your' life – for all the career opportunities and social activities that you might miss while your child is small. But never again will you have the opportunity to immerse your child in love, to be with him constantly and to experience all the joy and pleasure of watching him develop and grow.

At the risk of sounding sexist, and in no way making light of the many enlightened and committed fathers (believe me, I know some truly amazing full-time dads), I do say that Nature's design, perfected through the eons of the evolution of humankind and also a function, purely and simply of biology, ensures that mothers are gifted with the utmost tolerance, patience and sensitivity to their child's needs. Although this may be an unpopular sentiment today, it is worth remembering that there are rich and rare differences between men and women. It is also worth remembering that there is no more worthwhile job than raising children. Mothering is truly a job worth doing and it is worth doing well.

During those early, critically important years of your child's life, commit yourself totally to him. Nurse him, hold him, listen to him and share your life with him. The years when he is dependent are very short. If you put aside some of the scientific views of child-raising, you will develop a deeper emotional attachment with your child. You will be less likely to resent your crying baby, your immature toddler or your uncommunicative teenager. When you follow your instincts you can expect to experience more of the joy of child-raising and a lot less of the pain. And when you follow your intuition, both your child and the wider environment will benefit – for just as we have lost touch with our children, so we have lost touch with the earth.

If you give yourself unreservedly and wholeheartedly to this small person from his earliest days, you will be rewarded through all the years of his life with a loving and emotionally balanced individual. He will cope happily and adequately with an increasingly demanding world. He will be able to regain some sort of kinship with the earth and begin to treat it more kindly, and finally, in his turn he will be able to nurture his own children in exactly the same fashion when the time comes.

Now turn to 'Your action summary', a checklist for healthy bonding, breastfeeding and life with your toddler. If you have plans for another baby, read on.

## 4. Are you planning another baby?

If this book is your first introduction to the Healthy Parents, Healthy Baby Program and you want to prepare for another pregnancy, the following summary gives you the lowdown. For more details read *Healthy Parents, Healthy Baby*.

My passion for the preconception program grew from my work as a community pharmacist, which, after 15 years and frustration with band-aid medicine, had led me to a diploma in clinical nutrition. While engrossed in those studies, I became aware of Foresight, the UK-based Association for the Promotion of Preconceptual Care. It was their work that prompted the preparation I did before my own pregnancies and it was the benefits that I saw in every aspect of my baby-making years that inspired my crusade. The Foresight Association in the UK has carried out a huge amount of research, with

Professor David Barker from Southampton University's Developmental Origins of Health and Disease another leading light in this field.

But while the importance of the preconception period may come as a complete surprise to many couples, it's certainly not a new idea. Even the ancient Greeks and Romans knew that alcohol, drunk before and around the time of conception, was damaging to the foetus. They placed a ban on the drinking of alcohol by young women and newlyweds. Many tribal societies fed special diets to their young women (and young men) of child-bearing age. In the 1930s, American dentist Dr Weston Price studied communities from around the world and clearly established the link between the consumption of a refined Western diet and compromised health in the next generation outcomes.

The Great Dutch Famine at the end of World War Two showed that women exposed to the food shortages before and around the time of conception had poorer reproductive outcomes than the women who suffered food shortages during their pregnancy. And that's just the tip of the iceberg. The next generation was shown to be affected if the mother was in utero during the first trimester when her mother was exposed to food shortage. This finding introduces us to the exciting, emerging study of epigenetics. Research in this field demonstrates that the effects of deleterious physical and emotional traumas are carried down through generations, but what's really exciting is that the converse holds true, which is what makes this work so incredibly exciting and worthwhile!

What epigenetics shows is that there is an effect that goes beyond an individual's actual DNA profile. In fact 'epigenetics' literally means above or beyond genetics and it's exciting research – in 20 years it has turned conventional genetic wisdom on its head. That means we can no longer hold our DNA entirely responsible for our weight issues, heart disease, diabetes or whatever. We might have a genetic tendency to these or other conditions, but there is additional imprinting that can be both negative or positive, and there are triggers that can switch a genetic variation off or on. For example, new evidence indicates that the current epidemic of childhood obesity could in part be linked to the high-fat diet of the father-to-be.

So what preconception care endeavours to do is to remove any of those negative triggers and ensure that the positive ones only (and that includes positive mental and emotional effects) will ensure the healthiest possible egg and sperm and the healthiest possible environment for the developing embryo and, in that, the opportunity for the child to enjoy his full genetic potential.

For 30 years my passion has been promoting preconception health care as the way to improve fertility and to prevent miscarriage and other reproductive problems. But more importantly preconception health care is the logical, elegantly simple way to ensure a really beautiful, bright, happy, healthy baby.

And this preparation for pregnancy has never been more important than it is today. Infertility rates are on the rise, one woman in four will have a miscarriage, labours are frequently long and require medical intervention, breastfeeding periods are much too short and we have an epidemic of kids with subtle and not-so-subtle health issues. All of this represents a very inauspicious start to family life. For some, it represents a lifetime of heartache and hardship. Of course, the cost to the community and to healthcare systems is impossible to quantify.

But we can do something to reduce these issues. The story starts before conception and it starts with *both* prospective parents. This is about two people committing to giving their family the very best possible start in life and it's not really as hard as it sounds, nor as 'out there' as some might think.

In a nutshell 'preconception health care' means an abundance of all the basic building blocks: probiotics, vitamins, trace elements, essential fatty and amino acids, purified water and complete absence of anything that may be potentially toxic. Preconception health care must involve both partners equally and the program must be completed and in place for at least four months before conception. That doesn't mean 'cutting down on cigarettes' or 'reducing alcohol' during that critical four-month period. A smoking or drinking individual should have quit already because:

- Sperm take up to 116 days to form.
- Ova are susceptible to damage for 100 days prior to ovulation.

The bulk of what needs doing will involve your own actions, but sometimes you'll need help from a practitioner.

Let's talk for a moment about the basic building blocks. The primary source of these is a wholefood, organic diet. Stating it simply, that means healthy food grown on healthy soil, but that's often a tall order in today's society so supplements are important too. They can never take the place of the healthiest possible diet, but they're absolutely essential for both partners during that critical four-month period and for the pregnant and breastfeeding mum. That's not just any old multivitamin/mineral formulation, but products specifically designed for preconception, pregnancy and beyond. The longer you take this robust combination before conception, the better. The reasons for this are:

- Your needs during reproduction are so critical – a diet that may support adult life may be completely unable to support healthy reproduction.
- Time is short. (Most women hope to be pregnant yesterday, not tomorrow, and that's particularly the case if you're an older prospective mum.)
- You have to make up for multiple nutritional deficits caused by the years when you were eating a refined Western diet, enjoying unhealthy lifestyle habits and exposed to toxicity.

So a prospective mum needs a lot more than folic acid and iron, which are often the only nutrients prescribed by GPs and obstetricians. In fact, single nutrients are definitely not recommended. Folic acid, for example, is part of the B-complex group – it never occurs alone in nature and shouldn't be taken alone. Trace elements are important too.

You should assess and treat any zinc deficiency in the preconception period because zinc is the most important trace element if you're about to become pregnant. But zinc deficiency is also considered the most widespread deficiency in the Western world and that deficiency is almost entirely attributable to modern diets and lifestyles. Zinc is lost or destroyed by non-organic farming and refining of grains. Alcohol, cigarettes and diuretics (such as caffeine) all deplete your body of zinc. The detoxification of heavy metals such as lead requires zinc. Growth, pregnancy, breastfeeding, stress and illness all put increased demands on zinc levels. Finally, oral contraceptives as well as inorganic iron supplements seriously disturb zinc status!

Zinc deficiency has been implicated in the following (and keep in mind this list is not exhaustive):

- Low libido (no sex drive)
- Infertility
- Stretch marks
- Toxemia (high blood pressure during pregnancy)
- Poor foetal growth
- Premature birth
- Congenital defects
- Prolonged labour
- Postnatal (and antenatal) depression
- Cracked nipples
- Poor maternal instinct
- Irritable, jittery baby

- Compromised immunity
- Learning/behavioural problems

Surprised that prolonged labour can be partly attributable to a deficiency of a trace element? Well, zinc is intimately involved in collagen formation and in a zinc-deficient woman collagen formation is compromised, with gaps appearing in her uterine membrane. Those gaps mean that the uterus then contracts inefficiently – hence a long labour.

So how to restore your zinc levels? There's a very simple, inexpensive taste test for zinc status and it can be one of the first steps in a preconception program. Take 5 mL of a taste test solution in your mouth and swirl it around. Notice the sensation.

- A prompt strong, unpleasant taste is an optimal response and indicates adequate zinc levels.
- A dry mineral, sweet, furry or delayed taste or no taste indicates a moderate zinc deficiency.
- No specific taste indicates a strong zinc deficiency.

When you're done, supplement according to the zinc status revealed by the taste test. Simply follow the directions on the label, using a liquid product if your status is very compromised. And of course, remember you need all those other trace elements and vitamins too.

One of the major culprits in zinc deficiency is the oral contraceptive pill. The Pill causes copper levels to rise (copper is a zinc antagonist) and zinc levels to fall. It's often quite difficult to reverse zinc deficiency in long-term Pill users. So if you're on the Pill, make sure you have a really good break from it and restore your zinc status well ahead of any attempt at baby-making. Women who take the oral contraceptive pill right up to the time of conception will begin their pregnancy in a zinc-compromised state, with potential negative effects at every stage of their pregnancy and on their baby.

You may have been prescribed the Pill simply to regulate your cycles, but there is another way to do that. I'm dismayed when doctors prescribe the Pill for hormonal irregularities, because it only masks the problems and leads to more disturbances. Fortunately, there is a fabulous natural product that works to balance levels of all hormones across the board and it has full double-blind clinical trials to support its use. There's a companion product for men that improves sperm health and increases testosterone levels.

Appropriate water intake is another step in your preconception program. Purified water provides a primary detoxification measure and implementation of this one simple step – at least 2 litres of purified water every day – can make a big difference to how efficiently your body gets rid of toxic by-products. The best quality water will provide the optimal environment for every step of reproduction – from conception through to breastfeeding! I recommend a filtration system that actually restructures the water for optimal hydration and more efficient detoxification.

If water helps the body to detoxify, what toxicity should you be trying to avoid? We are all exposed to an absolute cocktail of chemicals – and there's no doubt of the potential for harm to eggs, sperm and a developing baby. I don't say this to alarm, but rather to alert you to the importance of avoiding whatever you can and to the importance of all of the protective measures that are available.

Let's consider the food supply – 20,000 chemicals are used in food production and manufacture and 4000 chemicals added directly to the food supply (but only 10 per cent are listed on labels). That's why you should aim to eat only healthy food grown in healthy soil.

Then consider common lifestyle habits. Alcohol is a direct testicular toxin and there is no known safe level of alcohol consumption during pregnancy. That's why I strongly recommend total avoidance of alcohol in the preconception period.

Then the personal care products in your bathroom (skin care, cosmetics, shampoos, etc.) are another source of toxic chemicals.

In fact, the average woman using 12 products daily will expose herself to 175 chemicals! Become a label reader and look for organic, chemical-free; some very clean/green products will contain only food-grade ingredients – they fit the bill perfectly in terms of toxicity-free skin care.

Heavy metals and electromagnetic radiation are other sources of toxicity that the preconception couple needs to be aware of. Keep mobiles out of pockets and laptops out of laps – away from reproductive organs.

The importance of thinking positively and reducing your stress levels can't be overemphasised. Taking time out for yourself with another child or children in the house can be difficult, but review Chapter 5: Think in *Healthy Parents, Healthy Baby* for some ideas on managing stress. The same goes for regular exercise – you may not be able to manage gym classes right now with a small child or children in your life, but regular exercise really doesn't have to take place in a structured environment.

# YOUR ACTION SUMMARY

✓ Optimise your nutrition – an adequate supply of all the vitamins, minerals, essential amino and fatty acids is necessary for labour and breastfeeding to proceed smoothly. Improve your diet and take a balanced combination of nutritional supplements. Choose specific support for pregnancy and breastfeeding.

✓ Make sure your diet contains an abundance of organically grown, fresh fruit and vegetables. If your intake isn't up to par, consider adding a 'greens' product. This is not a substitute for fresh produce in your diet, but a great way to include all those important phytochemicals that can support your positive dietary changes. Consumption of modern Western diets leads to an acidic pH in the body, but a slightly alkaline pH provides the optimal environment for fertility (and general wellbeing), with a fabulous diet and 'greens' providing help in this department as well.

✓ Take a good-quality probiotic. Choose one that contains multiple human strains – a premium variety will be many times more potent than conventional probiotics.

✓ Detoxify and hydrate – at least eight glasses of purified water every day (12 or more when you're breastfeeding) will help your body's natural detoxification processes. Look for a water filtration system that not only purifies but 'restructures' the water. This will also improve hydration and support transport of nutrients into the cells. A similar filter for your shower will reduce exposure to toxins such as chlorine.

✓ Avoid common social poisons such as cigarettes, alcohol, caffeine and other drugs (including oral contraceptives). Your supplementation program can help with cravings – take specifically designed products. Once your normal menstrual cycle returns but if you're still breastfeeding, avoid pharmaceutical contraception. NFM Contraception Kits tell you everything you need to know about swapping pharmaceutical or chemical contraception for easy-to-learn natural methods until you're ready to conceive again (or if your family is now complete).

✓ Avoid environmental toxicity. This means reducing your use of chemical-laden products and limiting your exposure to electromagnetic radiation. Organic, toxicity-free skin care is an excellent way to reduce the unhealthy chemical cocktail found in many skincare products.

✓ Check out protective devices that reduce exposure to EMR from your mobile phone and wireless connections – and use them!

✓ Establish a regular exercise routine – both aerobic conditioning and strength training are important. There are lots of fabulous options for regular exercise with a new baby or toddler in tow.

✓ Reduce stress. Thankfully, while you're breastfeeding, the hormones oxytocin and prolactin give you help in this area. Make sure you get as much sleep as you can, keep your baby within arm's reach at night-time and if you possibly can, nap during the day when your baby does.

✓ Sex is an effective stress-reduction tool but be aware that it may not be a regular stress-reducing remedy after the birth of your baby, particularly when you're breastfeeding. See 'Whatever happened to sex?' in Chapter 2 for the reasons why.

✓ In addition to reading this book and playing the game at www.flurishh.com, you might like to read my other titles with Francesca Naish, *The Natural Way to Better Birth and Bonding* and *The Natural Way to Better Breastfeeding*, for lots more information and advice.

✓ When you're ready to conceive again, continue with all of the above, but now support your foundation or core health. An adaptogenic product for both of you will restore hormone balance, support fertility and ensure that all of your ongoing health promotion measures achieve optimal results!

✓ Get help from a practitioner to treat any existing health conditions.

✓ Believe that everything you are doing can make the difference – an easy conception, healthy, full-term pregnancy, birth without medical intervention, prolonged breastfeeding, a beautiful, bright, happy, healthy baby and ongoing good health for your whole family. It's in your hands! You're smart, you've now got access to all the information and you've got an amazing opportunity. If you can do these things, within the framework of present Western culture, you're laying a rock-solid foundation for the physical, mental and emotional health of the next generation. They'll thank you for it for all of their lives!

# APPENDIX

## In your kitchen

Those readers who enjoyed Dave and Pauline's wonderful, creative recipes in *Healthy Parents, Healthy Baby* will be pleased to know that my family chefs are back – with a different style of recipe for a different style of cook!

As a teenager, Dave was rather fond of saying that 'mum rotated ten basic meals' which makes it remarkable that he has gone on to be part of the team in several award-winning kitchens and at the grand old age of 26 has established his own highly regarded and well-reviewed restaurant. Clearly something he learned at my knee must have made an impact. My preference for, and emphasis on, very simple but healthy fare, I can trace back to my family history . . .

It was the first decade of the twentieth century and doctors prescribed a move to Australia from the cold, damp and smog of Glasgow for the little girl who would become my grand-mother. Despite enjoying a much more agreeable climate in Sydney, Tibby remained incapacitated by severe asthma. Once she became a young mother she was almost unable to function, so in desperation, she consulted a naturopath. Back in the 1930s this was considered a remarkably daring move, but it was one that would have a dramatic impact. My grandmother lived out her 86 years in rude good health, completely asthma-free. The dramatic turnaround would also positively affect my mother's health as well as my own and certainly the course of my career.

Thanks to the naturopath's nutritional recommendations, my grandmother raised my mother on a raw, wholefood diet. In turn, my mother saw no reason for her daughters to be fed differently. The meals that she served up consisted largely of fresh vegetables and fruit, some wholemeal bread, cheese and fish, and a barbecue on Sundays provided our only red meat. Our diet was a daring model for its time. Mum used no table salt in her cooking and a cake made with wholemeal flour and raw sugar was an infrequent treat.

All our meals, including school lunches, were prepared at home from scratch. I was the only child at school who didn't drink the milk provided and who never ate the sandwiches from the canteen – even though I longed to try chocolate spread on white bread. For the school Christmas party, I secretly hoped that mum would bake cupcakes with blue icing and silver balls on top. Surprisingly, it was my own plate of brown bread and red salmon that always disappeared from the party table first. Today, children with salad vegies in their lunch boxes are commonplace, menus at school tuckshops have improved dramatically and healthy recipes have evolved beyond grated carrot and sunflower seeds (with all due respect to carrots and sunflowers), but in the early 1950s my diet was definitely considered weird.

Sydney University Union must also take some responsibility for this story. In 1964, at its refectory table I first became acquainted with the young Pharmacy student who was to become my partner of 30 years and father of our boys. My huge Tupperware bowls of fresh salad, lovingly prepared by a mother ever concerned for my wellbeing, consistently yielded up the capsicums, tomatoes and radishes that added zest to Alex's very different Hungarian diet and the grey Union offerings. Down the track he goaded me to learn more, when as a trained pharmacist, but one also reflecting my mum's teachings, I spoke of the 'goodness that was missing from modern diets'.

By the time I had two young sons at Montessori School, I was well and truly on the campaign trail that has occupied me for more than 30 years and the boys had benefited from my passion for the healthiest possible preconception, pregnancy and breastfeeding periods. Indeed, both boys were plucked rather reluctantly from said breast on their first days at preschool.

Just as my own early years played a strong part in my later life's path, maybe Dave will say the same for his career as a professional chef. While at his very first birthday party – a celebration for a fellow three-year-old – he was bewildered. Confronted by a table laden with sweet, sugary, multicoloured offerings, he cautiously reached for the only thing he recognised – sultanas. Three years down the track at a party for Dave himself – celebrating six and joined by his older Montessori classmates – I'd made the numeral '6' out of Smarties, as a birthday treat, sitting atop my specialty cake – a carrot and zucchini loaf. I knew Dave approved and when the slices disappeared in a flash, it proved to my enormous satisfaction that kids were not resistant to healthy food. The reality has become a standing family joke. On leaving the Botanical Gardens, there lay most of the cake, discarded in the garden bed, minus the Smarties!

My regular presentations to the Montessori parent body 'Food for Brains, Bodies and Behaviour' had positive effects on what parents included in their kids' lunch boxes, at least in the short term. The miracle is that my children's popularity didn't seem to suffer when their mates' crisps, muesli bars and chocolate frogs were replaced with real, living food.

Finally, Dave's contention that I had only ten meals in my repertoire may have been the straw that broke the camel's back. While the foundation of my work for the last 30 years is based on promoting healthier eating habits, my creative skills stop at the keyboard. The fact that one of my sons is enormously creative in the kitchen is a source of great delight – and a lot of memorable meals! So who or what to thank for that? Dave's prenatal exposure to healthy food, the early influence of lots of different tastes received courtesy of breastmilk, his involvement in the selection of only healthy food, my comments about the benefits of fresh, raw, uncontaminated as opposed to processed and refined, our family eating habits (at home or in restaurants), a combination of all of the above or something else entirely? Of course we'll never know, but together with his wife Pauline, they now focus on fresh, seasonal, local produce, organically grown or raised and combined in ways that are truly creative and appetising. If you've tried the recipes in *Healthy Parents, Healthy Baby*, I'm sure you'll agree.

So here, with a little help from this mum, we've chosen to revisit how Dave was exposed at home, at school and when eating out, to the selection, preparation and enjoyment of all manner of healthy, nutritious food. Pauline, who was an intrepid adventurer in her own mum's kitchen from her very earliest years, has weighed in with her suggestions for getting your kids involved in meal preparation. Hopefully our combined ideas will give your children the opportunity to become the masters of their own nutritional destiny – in the very best possible way!

## 1. Get them started young

A few words of advice before letting a child of any age loose in the kitchen.

## 2. Begin with simple steps

Here are some basic food selection and preparation activities to try.

## 3. Make the most of lunch boxes

Involve your child in selecting and preparing his lunch. The important thing here is to keep it fresh.

## 4. Ready for some recipes?

So now your child is ready for a recipe. Here's a healthy selection that should be within his capabilities.

## 5. For latecomers to healthy food selection and preparation

Time to revisit the general guidelines that can help you bring fresh, healthier ideas to family mealtimes.

# 1. Get them started young

A few words of advice before letting a child of any age loose in the kitchen:

- Supervision is required at all times. Remember, this exercise is about being there with your child just as much as it is about helping him to do it himself.
- Patience is another prerequisite. Make sure you have plenty of time for your kitchen activities, which should not only include preparation and consumption of the meal, but table-setting and cleaning up.
- While cleaning up is part of the whole process, and can be great fun for a child, don't worry about the inevitable mess or spillage along the way; it will all wash or wipe clean at the end. However, spills on the floor should be removed immediately so that the surface underfoot is always safe.
- A dry floor is just one elementary safety precaution; others should take into account any peculiarities of your particular kitchen or tendencies of your child.

Here are some other things to keep in mind.

- Make sure that long hair is tied away from your child's face.
- Long sleeves should be rolled up.
- Always insist on closed shoes with non-skid soles.
- Keep best clothes, fairy outfits and Batman capes out of the kitchen.
- Aprons are a great idea – choose ones with a bib front and made from cloth rather than plastic. Secure the ties with a double bow.
- Saucepan handles should always be turned towards the back of the stove.
- Make sure your child understands what parts of the oven and stove get hot.

- Insist that he always asks for help (or advice when older) if he wants to do something by himself.

- Any stool or booster step that is used to bring your child up to the right height for operating benchtop devices or the stove must be absolutely secure and slip-free.

- Don't force your child's involvement – and let him indicate when he's had enough. When he's very small it may be sufficient for him to measure and pour some of the ingredients, or perhaps to help set the table. Your kitchen activities should always be fun, not regimented.

- Make preparations in advance – just as travel with children will be more enjoyable with good advance planning, so too will your kitchen activities benefit if you think ahead and make the appropriate arrangements.

- Those arrangements should include a space where a very young child can begin his culinary adventures – so you'll need a child-sized table and chair that is securely positioned in a corner of the kitchen where it won't be in the way of other family members. This table and chair are for preparation, measuring, mixing and whatever else your child is able to do.

- For a very young child, a 'plug-in' seat that can be attached to a kitchen benchtop will give him a bird's-eye view of your activities (and the opportunity to help where appropriate). That means your kitchen bench or island needs free space (not cupboards) underneath and the seat should be safety-approved for the purpose. (Digressing a little, my boys were actually perched in one of these seats for all their early kitchen and dining experiences. From the time they were able to sit up, they were an integral part of all family mealtimes. As they grew bigger they graduated to a booster seat, but they were always part of food preparation or seated at the communal dining table. This seating arrangement gives a child the familiarity and confidence that is a vitally important part of his early eating experiences. He will see how food is prepared as well as what other members of his family are eating and he can copy what he observes. This is an entirely different experience from that of the child in an isolated highchair being spoon-fed when no one else around him is eating!)

- Child-size implements – not look-alike toys – are another important part of making the experience fun and educational for your child. With so much recent emphasis on children in the kitchen they are available, so shop around. Check Montessori sites too.

- Aim for beauty and order in preparation and presentation. This might seem like a complete oxymoron with a child who is just beginning his journey with food, but it's an important part of the eating experience. It shows him that mealtimes are an occasion and about a great deal more than just plonking food on a plate. So exactly how do you invoke beauty and order in the kitchen and during mealtimes?

— Avoid plastic implements wherever possible.

— Use glass or china bowls and measuring jugs. (There are plenty of robust unbreakable kinds.)

— Bring out the real china dinnerware. Perhaps even give your child a beautiful china dining setting? (I still have the lovely china cup that Dave chose for himself. It has survived the years – intact!)

— Favour table covers, placemats and napkins made of fabric rather than plastic or paper.

— Invest in a set of wooden or ceramic napkin rings. Different colours for different members of the family work well and a small child can easily include these in his table-setting activities.

— Always use your silver or stainless-steel cutlery. You'll probably have to buy some child-size spoons, forks and knives. If you are lucky enough to have real silver, your child will actually enjoy polishing it.

— Put a bunch of fresh flowers or herbs from your garden on the table.

— Include candles in the table-setting when your child is old enough to handle them safely.

— Finally, always make the food look attractive to eat (and look like food)!

## 2. Begin with simple steps

Here are some basic food selection and preparation activities to try. You can easily adapt them for your own kitchen, always keeping in mind what is of particular interest to your own child at any given moment.

- Measuring, pouring and cutting are simple, beginner activities that Montessori classrooms provide for very young children. When your child is small, these activities may be sufficient in themselves. However, they do provide good foundation activities that you can build on as your child's coordination, interest and ability improve and as he gains mastery of each.

- Your child should be seated at his own table and chair for these simple operations. The requisite pieces of equipment should have their own special tray which rests on an easily accessible shelf. Your child can collect the tray easily and get to work (just as he would do in the classroom).

- The tray should be set with a cloth placemat together with a small glass dish or bowl, which contains the item to be measured. (Rice, couscous, quinoa, dried beans or lentils are great for this activity.) Alongside place a spoon and a measuring jug. The idea is for your child to spoon the ingredients from the bowl into the jug. He will probably want to repeat this multiple times until he's 'got it'.

- You can arrange a similar set-up for learning to pour, which doesn't necessarily have to involve a liquid – various varieties of small seeds can provide good pouring practice.

- Your child can then progress to spooning or pouring some dried fruit, nuts or seeds into a container, making them ready for instant snacks, which of course he might well eat during preparation time.

- A similar activity provides a pair of blunt tweezers, allowing one piece of food at a time to be placed in a bowl or jar. This encourages hand–eye coordination and fine motor control, as well as healthy food choices.

- At the organic fruit market, your child can help name and choose the fruit varieties. When you come home, he can arrange the various pieces in a bowl and select one for his snack.

- Then he can cut the fruit. Show him how to make a bridge with his fingers and put the knife underneath the bridge. Choose a small, but real knife that is actually capable of cutting – a blunt one might seem like a safer option, but it won't work. A child from about three years of age can cut fruit confidently with an experienced helping hand at the cutting board. Celery also lends itself well to this activity as do other raw vegetables, such as broccoli or cauliflower, although you should always ask for your vegies and fruit to be cut just prior to use, which will mean less loss of nutritional content.

- The cut fruit or vegetable is then ready to eat or you might like to involve your child in making a smoothie. He can add the fruit to the blender jug, then pour some water, yoghurt, seeds or whatever on top. He can put the lid on and press the start button. Make sure he understands that blades are sharp, that the lid must be properly secured and that electrical appliances should never be operated without his mum or dad's supervision. Also make sure he gets to try some of the contents!

- In the fridge, you can make sure that vegies such as cherry tomatoes, snow peas, green beans and button mushrooms are on readily accessible shelves. All make great raw snacks. See below for dip ideas to go with these crudités.
- Other food preparation could involve your child in shelling peas, topping and tailing beans or scrubbing root vegetables. I recommend against peeling things like potatoes and kumera, since so much of the nutritional value then goes into the compost along with the skins. A small nailbrush and a bowl of water are all that small hands need to remove the dirt ready for cooking.

## Move to the stove

Once you consider that your child has mastered the basics, here are some more adventurous activities he can try. Gaining confidence with cooking means starting with simple things that will produce the desired result every time.

- A child can easily boil eggs (an eggtimer is a wise investment) and cook cobs of corn.
- Toasting bread, crumpets or muffins is a no-brainer. Keep the butter out of the fridge so that spreading doesn't ruin the success of the toasting process, or try other spreads (see ideas below).
- Lunch boxes are well within your child's capabilities and more likely to get eaten when he's been involved in the preparation. (Great ideas for these to follow.)
- Toasted sandwiches in a special sandwich maker can become real works of art once kids start getting creative with the

ingredients. Leftovers won't last long once hungry sandwich makers know how to operate this device.

- Brown rice is a good example of foolproof food. It's then ready to mix with sweet things such as fruit, which might be freshly cut or perhaps stewed ahead of time with sultanas or a little honey. Add some yoghurt. Alternatively, mix the rice with savoury foods such as tuna, chopped tomatoes, shallots, Spanish onion or chives, all enhanced with a dash of tamari. Whatever the preferred combination, it will give your child the sense of serving up a complete dish for the family – one that he has prepared all by himself!

- As another starting point at the stove, a child can be offered the task of browning onions or other vegetables for soups or casseroles, but keeping the stove on a low heat is a good idea until he becomes familiar with the change in texture and appearance and the potential to burn.

- Once both of you are comfortable with the operation of gas burners, hot plates and the oven – all of which will require your supervision for some considerable time – the next steps are really as varied or repetitive, as simple or as complex as your child indicates he's up for. Now it's a wonderful dance in the kitchen, hopefully with all family members involved in the creation of meals, just as you will all be involved in their consumption.

- When your child is finally ready to follow a recipe, guide him towards ones you've made before and the outcome of which you can guarantee. Success in following step-by-step instructions will build kitchen confidence and the enthusiasm to embark on new and different creations. By then your child will probably be old enough to understand that a new recipe may not always deliver the desired result – the secret is to remain endlessly supportive and positive about his offerings.

The last thing you want is for a less than optimal outcome to signal the end of your child's culinary experiments.

## Setting up and cleaning up

When your child is just a beginner, washing up can actually be an exciting and satisfying activity all by itself, just as can table-setting. Keep the beauty and order rule in mind when guiding a small child through setting the table. The same small table and chair can be used for washing up, which obviously should be limited to robust glassware and blunt utensils. Cloth napkins can provide washing practice too.

## Little green fingers

Whether it's a small pot on your windowsill or balcony, or a backyard garden with a worm farm and compost bin, gardening is a hugely satisfying activity for the whole family. An understanding of where food comes from, encouraged by planting, picking and eating home-grown produce is really important – considering that a national survey by the Australian Council for Educational Research in 2012 found that 27 per cent of Australian primary school children believe that yoghurt grows on trees! *Healthy Parents, Healthy Baby* is a good starting point for introducing your child to gardening.

## Sprouts

Bean sprouts are highly nutritious – and they're also easy for kids to grow. Soy, mung and peas are good choices; you could also try wheat or rye. You'll need a container with a cover and small holes in the bottom for drainage. There are of course special sprouting trays, but you can also modify something you already have in the kitchen. Just make sure your chosen tray is big enough – the sprouting beans swell and will occupy considerably more space than dry beans. Soak the beans in purified water overnight, spread evenly on the tray then rinse well with running water twice daily. Kids will love watching the sprouting process and the sprouts will be ready to eat in four or five days. Don't sprout too many at a time; they taste better when eaten in their prime and can be added to salads or stir-fries. Alternatively, pop a handful into a lunch box.

## 3. Make the most of lunch boxes

Involve your child in selecting and preparing his lunch. The important thing here is to keep it fresh. Thankfully, lunch boxes now feature insulated linings and special freezer bricks for safe and convenient storage. Choose a well-designed item, so food lovingly prepared in the morning will still be crisp and attractive when it's opened.

## Pack the protein

Start with protein and build around it. Protein is an important part of any meal or snack, often the hardest thing to include and to keep fresh. The protein inclusion will depend on the age of the child and on their ability to manage bones or to open a can.

Here are some ideas:

- Roasted or barbecued chicken drumsticks
- Roasted or marinated chicken wings
- Slice of roast lamb, beef, chicken
- Barbecued sausage
- Bean dip – combined with grains (e.g., corn chips or pita bread)
- Can of tuna
- Boiled egg
- Slice of homemade pizza, frittata, quiche or Spanish omelette
- Nut spread/nut butter. (Note, however, that peanut butter is a common source of allergy and it's quite likely that it will be a banned substance at your child's school.)

## Add the vegetable rainbow

Include a small container of dip (see 'All into the blender' below) to make vegies more interesting. Leave the vegetables whole wherever possible or cut into large chunks.

The following are good choices:

- Beans
- Capsicum
- Carrots
- Cauliflower
- Celery
- Cherry tomatoes
- Cucumber
- Lettuce – leaf variety
- Mushrooms
- Peas
- Radishes
- Snowpeas
- Tomatoes

## Cooked vegetables

The following are delicious when lightly steamed:

- Asparagus
- Beans
- Corn on the cob
- Snowpeas

If you like, include a container of dipping sauce.

The following do well roasted in coconut oil the night before. They're great to eat cold and can be dipped in a small container of mixed seeds that have been toasted in tamari – you can easily prepare this mix yourself or look for a commercial product.

- Capsicum
- Corn on the cob
- Eggplant
- Kumera
- Potato
- Pumpkin
- Zucchini

## Fabulous fruit

While sliced fruit may look attractive and appear easy to manage when it's freshly cut, by lunchtime it may have lost its original appeal. It will certainly have lost a lot of its nutritional value. Aim to include fresh, whole fruit, but make sure it's a size that is manageable for your child. Also make sure that your child can handle pipped fruit, such as cherries.

Here are some suggestions:

- Apricots
- Bananas
- Blueberries
- Cherries
- Figs
- Grapes (seedless)
- Mandarins
- Peaches
- Plums
- Strawberries

## Bread and other grains

Choose from the following options:

- Artisan bread (or see *Healthy Parents, Healthy Baby* for Pauline's easy-to-make Bread for Beginners)

- Wholemeal rolls
- Wholegrain bread
- Pita bread
- Lebanese bread
- Crisp bread
- Rice or corn cakes
- Pumpernickel (for older children)
- Organic unsalted corn chips
- Blue corn chips (delicious and a change from yellow corn)
- Brown rice salad
- Pasta salad

## Spreads, dips and dressings

Following are some suggestions for spreads, dips and dressings to try:

- Organic butter
- Nut butters (not peanut)
- Avocado – mix mashed avocado with lemon or lime juice to prevent browning
- Make your own dip using ricotta, cream cheese or yoghurt as a base. Add chopped chives, Spanish onion, shallots or mashed avocado
- Basic Salad Dressing – see 'Staples for the fridge' below
- Beetroot, carrot, hummus – see 'All into the blender' below

## 4. Ready for some recipes?

So now your child is ready for a recipe. Here's a healthy selection that should be within his capabilities. Some may require a bit of help from mum or dad depending on age and culinary skills.

Remember, choose organic ingredients wherever possible. Eggs should be from free-range, organically fed hens; olive oil, organic, cold pressed, extra virgin; pepper, freshly ground, black; salt, Original Himalayan Crystal Salt, sea or Celtic salt (not common table salt).

# All into the blender

## Sweet smoothie

For a snack or a sweet treat, your child can try making a mango, raspberry and banana smoothie. You can substitute the flesh of other soft fruits depending on what's in season. The following quantities make two large serves.

1 large banana
1 punnet fresh raspberries (or 150 g of frozen raspberries)
flesh from one ripe mango (cut off the cheeks, score the flesh into
    cubes with a knife, then scoop out with a spoon)
1 cup ice cubes
½ cup unsweetened yoghurt
honey to taste (optional)

Put all in a blender and whiz!

# Dips

The perfect accompaniment to all those raw vegies that your little chef has chopped. Crudités, as they are sometimes known, with a dip that is equally nutritious also make great snacks and are good in lunch boxes. When you're not confined to what's on the supermarket shelves you can try any number of interesting combinations. They can also be used as a clever way to include any vegies that may not be on your child's very favourite list. Experiment, but try these for starters.

### Beetroot dip

425 g can of good-quality beetroot
(Alternatively you can use 8 fresh baby beetroots or 2 large beetroots,
    steamed until soft)
2–3 tbsp Greek yoghurt
olive oil
lemon juice

1. In a food processor, roughly chop the beetroot.
2. Add the yoghurt, a splash of olive oil and a squeeze of lemon
   juice.
3. Blend until smooth.
4. Adjust to taste and season with salt and pepper.

(For carrot dip, steam carrots until they are tender and follow the
same method. Other cooked vegies can be used creatively too.)

### Hummus

1 can organic chickpeas, drained and rinsed well
2 gloves garlic, thinly sliced (use more if the kids will agree – garlic
    has great antibacterial and detoxifying properties)
1 tbsp organic tahini paste (start with 1 tbsp and adjust to suit your
    child's taste)
juice of 2 lemons
olive oil

1. Sauté garlic in olive oil in a medium-sized saucepan until really
   soft.
2. Add drained chickpeas and warm through.
3. Transfer to blender or food processor, then add tahini paste, a
   good splash of olive oil and the lemon juice.
4. Season with sea salt and pepper.

5. Blend and check consistency. This is a matter of taste – add another dash of oil or some filtered water if you find that it is too thick, and blend again.

## Some staples for your fridge

Preparing some of your regular stand-bys provides another chance for a small child to feel proud of his kitchen activities. Every time he opens the fridge he can see the bottle or jar of whatever he has made. Find some labels and ask your child to name the product. He might be able to create a colourful logo for 'Pauline's Pesto' or 'Dave's Salad Dressing', substituting his own name. Always include the date of production on the label.

### Pauline's Pesto
1 bunch fresh basil
2 tbsp toasted pine nuts
3 tbsp freshly grated parmesan cheese
olive oil

1. Place the basil leaves, pine nuts and parmesan in a blender or food processor.
2. Blend, and add enough olive oil to achieve a thick sauce consistency.
3. Season with sea salt and pepper.

### Dave's Basic Salad Dressing
250 mL lemon juice
750 mL extra virgin olive oil
125 g caster sugar (optional, but a little sugar really does makes the dressing so much better tasting. If you do choose to include sugar, you might like to know that your sugar intake in 1 tablespoonful of dressing is approximately 3 g (½ tsp))
1 clove garlic

1. Combine lemon juice and caster sugar in a bowl.
2. Whisk until sugar is dissolved.
3. Crush garlic clove lightly (just enough to release flavour) and add to the mix.
4. Once sugar is dissolved, add the olive oil.
5. Keep in the fridge but bring to room temperature before use. Shake or stir well to emulsify before dressing your salad.

(Makes 1 litre of dressing)

## Homemade breadcrumbs

Stale or fresh bread, sliced

1. Leave sliced, stale bread to dry in the air.
2. If you are using fresh bread, dry bread in the oven at a low temperature.
3. Placed the dried bread in your food processor and chop to achieve the consistency you desire.
4. Store in an airtight container (not in the fridge).

# Salads

Below are some basic salad ideas that are both super nutritious and simple for kids to assemble. All are good starters for giving your young chef the satisfaction of preparing a whole dish himself and are perfect for light lunches or filling snacks. They can also serve as accompaniments to more ambitious dinners. Let the whole family try devising their own favourite salad combos. Quantities can be varied depending on numbers to be fed and on favourite or readily available ingredients. All will be enhanced with the addition of the Basic Salad Dressing that your chef has already prepared.

- Grated carrot, finely shredded cabbage (red or white), chopped capsicum, tasty cheese (grated), finely chopped Spanish onion (optional)

- Diced celery, diced red apple, sultanas and finely chopped hazelnuts or walnuts
- Roast beetroot, grated carrot, toasted pepitas and crumbled feta
- Diced celery, green grapes, raisins and finely chopped walnuts
- Small florets of cauliflower, chopped celery, watercress, toss with mixed seeds roasted in tamari
- Sliced zucchini, super finely sliced fennel, dill, lemon juice – marinate and add crumbled feta

You might also wish to include some of the following: cooked lentils or chickpeas, barley, quinoa, lightly steamed snowpeas, green beans, finely chopped onion or shallot, mint, parsley, basil, rocket.

## Eggs

### French toast

French toast is a favourite in many households, including my own! My family still turn up on a Sunday morning and devour as many rounds as I can serve up. Two- to three-day-old bread works best – suggest using a good sourdough or white bread (an exception) for this recipe. Calculate two to three pieces of toast each for adults and bigger kids and one for littlies. The following quantities serve four hearty appetites.

8 large rounds of bread – lie them flat in an oven-proof dish (you might need two)
4 eggs
½ cup organic milk
1 tsp vanilla essence
2 tsp sugar

Accompaniments:
2 large bananas, sliced
1 punnet strawberries, sliced
1 punnet blueberries
mascarpone
maple syrup

1. Whisk eggs, milk, sugar and vanilla until well mixed.
2. Pour over the bread and make sure all slices are well coated.
3. Leave to stand – the egg mixture will soak into the bread.
4. Heat some butter in a pan over medium heat.
5. Cook the bread slices until golden brown on both sides.
6. Serve with fruit, syrup and a dollop of mascarpone.

*Scrambled eggs*
eggs, two per person
organic cream (optional)
small handful of mixed chopped fresh herbs, e.g. parsley, chives,
    chervil or tarragon
organic butter

1. Beat the eggs and cream in a small bowl, season with sea salt and
   pepper.
2. Melt a small knob of butter in a non-stick pan (it's okay to use
   non-stick for eggs) and melt till the butter starts foaming.
3. Pour in the egg mix and cook over a moderate heat, stirring
   continuously.
4. Remove from heat before completely cooked (eggs will be still a
   bit runny).
5. Serve with some toasted sourdough and sprinkle with herbs.

For a more substantial breakfast add your favourites – tomatoes,
mushrooms, avocado, bacon or smoked salmon.

## Fish

Find a reliable fishmonger whose wares are always fresh. Look for bright eyes and red gills.

### Fish fingers

600 g white-fleshed fish, such as flathead, ling or blue-eye cod. Ask your fishmonger to remove all skin and bones and cut into 50 g chunks

1 cup plain flour

3 eggs, whisked

1½ cups breadcrumbs (see recipe above)

1 cup Greek yoghurt

1 bunch dill

lemon juice

olive oil

### For the coating:

1. Coat fish pieces lightly in flour then pat off any excess.
2. Dip in egg mixture.
3. Then dip in breadcrumbs until well coated on both sides.

### For the accompaniment:

1. In a bowl add the yoghurt, dill, lemon juice (to taste) and olive oil. Mix until well combined.

### Cooking:

1. Bake coated fish pieces in oven until golden brown or pan-fry in skillet on medium heat.

(Serves 4)

### Fish cakes

3 medium Desirée potatoes, cut into chunks with skins left on

200 g hot* smoked trout or salmon, flaked (*refers to cooking/ smoking process)

1 bunch dill, roughly chopped

½ bunch shallots, finely chopped

zest of 1 lemon

zest of 1 lime

1 cup plain flour

3 eggs, whisked

1½ cups breadcrumbs (see recipe above)

*For the patties:*
1. Steam potatoes until tender then mash them.
2. Set aside until they are cool enough to touch but not cold.
3. Add trout or salmon, dill, shallots, lemon and lime zest and mix well with your hands.
4. Shape and flatten to make small palm-sized patties.
5. Put in the fridge to cool.

*For the coating:*
1. Coat fish cakes lightly in flour then pat off any excess.
2. Dip in egg mixture.
3. Then dip in breadcrumbs until well coated on both sides.

*Cooking:*
1. Pan-fry on medium heat until golden brown on both sides. (Remember that everything inside is already cooked.)

*To serve:*
Serve with some yoghurt or a dressed green salad. The more adventurous may wish to try a shaved fennel and rocket salad.
(Serves 6 people – 2 fish cakes each)

# Meat

## *Beef and vegetable skewers*

300 g rump steak or scotch fillet (will be more tender), cut into bite-size pieces

a selection of vegies, cut into bite size pieces

(These could include button mushrooms, red, yellow or green capsicum, zucchini or Spanish onion)

bamboo or metal skewers

1. Thread meat and vegetables alternately (varying the colours) on a skewer or kebab stick.

## *For the marinade:*

½ bunch rosemary

1 clove garlic

olive oil

1. In a mortar and pestle pound rosemary and garlic, drizzle olive oil to make a paste.
2. Use a pastry brush to coat kebabs and leave for one hour.
3. Barbecue on a hot plate, turning constantly.

## *To serve:*

Serve with yoghurt, lemon wedge and a green salad.

## *Lamb kofta (meatballs)*

½ kg lamb mince

2 brown onions, finely chopped

2 cloves garlic, minced

1 tbsp ground coriander

1 tbsp ground cumin seeds

1 tbsp ground fennel seeds

1 pinch dried chilli flakes (optional)
½ bunch parsley, finely chopped
½ bunch coriander, finely chopped
100 g toasted pine nuts
1 egg, whisked
olive oil

1. Sautée onion and garlic in olive oil until soft.
2. Add ground spices and cook over medium heat for 2–3 minutes.
3. Remove from heat and allow to cool.
4. In a big bowl, add onion and garlic, lamb mince and remaining ingredients.
5. Get your hands in the bowl and mix until everything is well combined.
6. Season with salt and pepper and mix again.
7. Form little meatballs or burger-shaped patties – cook in an oiled skillet until done to your liking. (For variety, you may wish to mould into a sausage shape around a wooden skewer and cook on the barbecue.)

(Makes 20 meatballs)

### To serve:
Serve with hummus or other dip or with stuffed mushrooms (see recipe below) for a more substantial meal. If you've made patties, serve on a bun with traditional hamburger accompaniments.

### Asian poached chicken with coleslaw
2 chicken breasts
¼ head cabbage (green, Chinese or Savoy), finely shredded
2 large carrots, grated
½ Spanish onion, finely sliced
½ bunch mint, finely chopped

½ bunch coriander, finely chopped

¼ cup roasted peanuts

4 tbsp toasted sesame seeds

juice of 3 limes

2 tsps demerara sugar

2 tsps sesame oil

*For the dressing:*

1. Place lime juice in a bowl, dissolve sugar and mix in sesame oil.
2. Adjust to your taste.

*Cooking:*

1. Trim chicken breasts of fat and sinew.
2. Place in lightly simmering water and poach very gently until cooked all the way through.
3. Remove from water and cool to room temperature.
4. When chicken is cool, slice finely.
5. In a large bowl, mix all salad ingredients, including chicken.
6. Add dressing and season with salt and pepper.

(Serves 4)

# Vegetables

*Vegetable and pasta salad*

Most kids love pasta, but here's a way to include those all-important red, orange, green and purple vegetables at the same time.

1 packet dried pasta (your child can choose his favourite shape – not spaghetti – for this recipe. *Fusilli* (spirals), *orecchiette* (ears), *penne* (tubes), *ruotine* (wheels) are all good for salads and he can learn the Italian names)

vegetables, raw or cooked, or a combination of both, served in strips or bite-sized chunks. (Try bite-size pieces of roast pumpkin or roast eggplant, shaved fennel, raw or roasted cherry tomatoes) selection of herbs (e.g. parsley, dill, basil, chives), finely chopped goat's cheese, feta or parmesan

1. Cook pasta in boiling, salted water for the recommended time.
2. Drain and refresh under cold water to stop the cooking.
3. Toss in a small amount of olive oil so the pasta shapes won't stick together.
4. Mix vegetables and herbs together, add crumbled goats cheese, fetta or parmesan.
5. Toss through the cool pasta and dress with Dave's Basic Salad Dressing.

### Oven-roasted chips

These can accompany meat, chicken or fish. A perennial favourite, but much healthier than the commercial, deep-fried varieties.

Starchy potatoes, e.g. Desirée, kipfler, or Royal Blue. (Kumera makes an interesting change, or you can try a mixture of both. Suggest one large potato per large person, less for littlies but more for hearty eaters.)
Olive or coconut oil (a particularly healthy choice)

1. Slice or dice the potatoes.
2. Toss in a baking pan with olive or coconut oil.
3. Season with salt and pepper.
4. Roast in a hot oven until cooked through.

### Stuffed mushrooms

For 6 mushrooms (one per person):
6 large field mushrooms, stalks removed
1 large brown onion, finely chopped
1 clove garlic, minced
2 rashers bacon (rind removed), finely chopped

250 g cooked couscous (follow directions on packet)
100 g toasted pine nuts
½ bunch parsley, finely chopped
zest of 1 lemon
butter
olive oil

1. Melt butter in a saucepan and sweat onion and garlic in the butter until soft.
2. Combine all ingredients and mix well.
3. On a large baking tray, arrange mushrooms upside down.
4. Place a knob of butter on each and season with salt and pepper.
5. Divide mix evenly between mushrooms and pack it down well.
6. Drizzle with olive oil.
7. Roast in a moderate oven at 180°C for 20–25 minutes or until mushrooms are tender.

Serve as an entrée or as a main with green salad.

You can use the same mix for capsicums or eggplant. For stuffed eggplant, cut large eggplants in half, score the flesh in a crisscross pattern, baste with olive oil and roast until soft. Scoop out the cooked flesh and add to the stuffing mix before packing back into the shells.

## Pizza dough

Pizzas are not only great fun for kids to make as it gives them a true 'hands-on' experience, but they can be creative with healthy toppings that are much lower in sodium chloride and saturated fat than those offerings from fast-food outlets or the supermarket freezer. We estimate this following recipe will make about 6–7 pizza pockets (calzone) or a smaller number of medium-sized flat pizzas. Of course, some of the dough can be frozen for later.

1½ sachets dried yeast (store remainder of sachet in fridge)

15 g sugar

310 mL tepid water (measure this accurately)

500 g plain flour

15 g salt

tomato puree

mozzarella, grated

a selection of toppings and herbs

1. Dissolve yeast and sugar in water.
2. Let stand for 2–3 minutes to activate the yeast.
3. On a large clean workbench (or in a big bowl if you have limited bench space), mix the salt and flour and make a well in the middle.
4. Slowly pour in the water mixture.
5. Incorporate it with your hands, bringing the flour in from the outside until all combined.
6. Now knead the dough for 5 minutes, adding a little extra flour if necessary.
7. Continue until the dough is elastic. (Kids love this part – they can pretend to be the professional at the local pizzeria.)
8. Put elastic dough in a lightly oiled bowl and cover with a tea towel. Leave for 1 hour.

After this time the dough should have doubled in size.

9. Now knock out the air (punch down the dough). (Kids love doing this too.)
10. If not all the dough is required, divide into two portions and freeze half for later use.
11. Roll out the remaining dough on a floured workbench and cut to the desired shape or size.
    Small, medium, large, round or square. This will depend on what size pizza tray you have.

12. Toppings or fillings we'll leave up to you – the possibilities are endless but start with tomato puree and grated mozzarella cheese and go from there.

13. Cook in the hottest oven you can manage – at least 220°C.

## Sweet treats

### Pauline's Sweet Slice (or Sprinkle)

200 g rolled oats

2 tbsp shredded coconut

2 tbsp pepitas

2 tbsp sunflower seeds

2 tbsp sesame seeds

2 tbsp slivered almonds

handful dried cranberries

90 g unsalted butter

¼ cup extra virgin olive oil

75 g raw caster sugar

75 g your favourite honey

1. Preheat oven to 180°C.
2. Line a medium-sized baking tray with baking paper.
3. Heat a saucepan on medium heat.
4. Add the butter, olive oil, sugar and honey and stir to combine.
5. Heat until just bubbling and the sugar has dissolved.
6. Mix the remaining ingredients in a large bowl and add the hot syrup to the bowl. Stir well to ensure all ingredients are coated.
7. Pour the mixture into the prepared tray and push the mixture firmly down to bind all ingredients together. (This will help the slices hold their shape once cooked.)
8. Place in the oven and bake for 10 minutes.
9. Turn the heat down to 150°C, cook for another 10–20 minutes, or until nicely toasted.

10. Remove from the oven and let cool for at least 40 minutes before you slice.
11. Keep slices in an airtight container for up to 3 weeks.

(Makes approximately 12 slices.)

This is a wonderfully adaptable recipe, a much healthier option than commercial muesli bars, and you can vary the ingredients, creating an endless variety of nut, seed and grain combinations, including chia seeds, linseed, currants, dates, walnuts, rice puffs, sultanas, dried figs, peanuts (remember, of course, that some children may be allergic) and chocolate chips (for a special treat).

As an alternative, you can crumble Pauline's Sweet Slice over a fruit and yoghurt dessert. For a party or special occasion you could try layering the fruit, yoghurt and crushed slice in tall parfait glasses.

### Banana bread (or muffins)
2 bananas, overripe and soft
100 g butter
100 g raw/caster sugar
1 tsp vanilla
½ tsp cinnamon
2 eggs
2 cups plain flour
3 tsp baking powder

1. Preheat oven to 180°C.
2. Grease a loaf tin.
3. Melt butter and place in a large mixing bowl.
4. Add sugar, vanilla, cinnamon and eggs and whisk to combine.
5. Mash bananas and add to wet ingredients.
6. Mix the baking powder and flour and sieve.
7. Add to wet ingredients and fold through.

8. Pour mix into loaf tin

9. Bake for 20–30 min until a skewer comes out clean.

(For muffins, pour mixture into greased muffin tray and reduce cooking time.)

## 5. For latecomers to healthy food selection and preparation

Time to revisit the general guidelines that can help you bring fresh, healthier ideas to family mealtimes. They'll stand you in good stead to encourage the eating habits that can lead to a lifetime of better physical and mental health down the track – and even to better health for your children's children.

### Healthy eating habits for the family

✓ Plan ahead and shop for the menus. We've already provided a small selection that are appropriate for family meals. If you don't buy those unhealthy 'impulse' foods, your child can't eat them.

✓ When making changes to eating habits don't try to make them all at once.

✓ Begin with breakfast to promote your child's ability to learn. Just make sure it's a balanced breakfast. Most children (and adults for that matter) start the day with too many simple carbohydrates and insufficient protein. Cereal manufacturers can take the blame here – especially the ones where sugar makes up a bigger proportion of the cereal than grain.

✓ Get to work on those lunch boxes. Remember to choose a well-insulated box with a freezer brick so that food will stay fresh.

### Shopping

✓ Buy as much as you can from your organic supplier. High levels of pesticides may be consumed when eating fruit and vegetables grown by non-organic methods.

✓ Make sure that your family gets the recommended daily intake of five serves of vegetables and two fruit. (That should be seven serves of vegies and five fruit when you're breastfeeding.)

✓ The best source of trace elements, antioxidants and phyto-chemicals, including anthocyanins, carotenoids, flavonoids and sulphides, are vegies and fruit. Remember to 'eat a rainbow every day'.

✓ Shop when you're well fed (and when you're child's well fed if he shops with you).

✓ Go to a wholefood supermarket – they don't display confectionery beside the cash register. Let him pick the appropriate, healthy items off the shelves.

✓ Read labels. Be aware of all the different names for sugar, e.g., glucose, dextrose, sucrose, fructose, maltose, mannose, lactose, corn starch, honey, maltodextrin, molasses, malt, sorbitol, etc. In particular avoid high-fructose corn syrup (HFCS) and artificial sweeteners. Remember that the doses of sugar, preservatives, colourings and so on that you can tolerate provide a relatively large dose per kilogram of body weight for a child.

✓ Particularly avoid foods that contain red and orange colouring (tartrazine), which increases the excretion of zinc which is needed for brain function.

## Menus

✓ Sweet tastes are inherently pleasing. Use organically grown and sun-dried dates or figs in moderation to satisfy your child's sweet tooth. Boil them to get rid of the mould that collects on their skins. Use honey sparingly.

✓ Avoid using common table salt to flavour food. Use a salt product that also contains trace minerals.

✓ Avoid over-dependence on grains. (Although grains are useful foods, they're over-represented in Western diets.

Wheat is also much less nutritious than it used to be – thanks to non-sustainable farming and the breeding for specific characteristics, wheat now contains as little as 10 per cent protein. In the 1950s it was as high as 90 per cent.) Try some different grains, such as couscous, quinoa, barley and buckwheat.

✓ If your child decides to take up a vegetarian diet (often the dietary choice of teenage girls), make sure that diet includes lots of variety and adequate protein. Vegetarians should go easy on the high-fibre foods (especially cereals) since they can inhibit the absorption of essential nutrients. Avoid convenience foods and do not let vegetarianism become an excuse not to eat. More on combining vegetable protein types in *Healthy Parents, Healthy Baby*.

## Cooking

✓ Favour dry-baking, steaming or stir-frying.

✓ Try herbs, lemon juice and other seasonings to add flavour.

✓ When baking cakes or desserts, substitute wholemeal for white flour (and sweeten with boiled dried fruits if appropriate). Add mashed or grated carrot, zucchini, pumpkin, banana, etc., to cakes.

✓ Avoid microwaving. Even though it's very convenient (especially for those child-sized portions that you've frozen), microwaved food undergoes molecular damage and can cause changes in human blood and immune systems.

## Eating

✓ Don't use food as a bribe. In particular, don't equate sweets or chocolate with rewards.

✓ When you do give your toddler a treat, or when your resolve crumbles, give him a child-sized portion.

✓ If sweet things get eaten first, they are often all that gets eaten.

✓ Make food look attractive. Experiment with contrasting colours and fun arrangements.

✓ Make sure your toddler eats often and little, rather than infrequently and lots. Too much food at one time can overload his digestive system, and too long between meals can encourage unhealthy snacks.

✓ Have those healthy snacks on hand always. Choose organically grown carrot, cucumber or celery sticks, button mushrooms, cherry tomatoes, rice cakes or crackers and wholegrain bread. Use dried fruit (including sultanas) sparingly.

✓ Try hummus, guacamole and taramasalata dips.

✓ Nuts or seeds shouldn't be given before your child is two (to avoid choking) but you might like to try nut butters. Think cashew and sesame seed (tahini) instead of the old faithful peanut. These should be kept in the fridge so the oil doesn't go rancid.

✓ Due to the risk of allergy, it's recommended that peanuts (and products containing peanuts such as peanut butter) not be given until your child is five. (The source of this allergy is actually the mould found on the broken and crushed peanuts that are used to make peanut butter. The better quality, whole nuts, which are less likely to be mouldy, make their way into jars and packets.)

✓ Pre-cook some brown rice and keep it in the fridge. This mixes well with sweet or savoury foods.

✓ Have good-quality, organic wholegrain bread available at all times. See *Healthy Parents, Healthy Baby* for Pauline's foolproof Bread for Beginners.

## Drinking

✓ Choose purified water, not fruit juices.

✓ Drink between meals, not with them.

✓ Avoid all soft drinks – they contain sugar, caffeine and worse.

To finish, I will quote Michael Pollan, author of *In Defense of Food: An Eater's Manifesto*. Pollan went back to the wisdom of the village and asked the 'tribe', readers of *The New York Times*, for their rules about healthy, enjoyable eating. Pollan received more than 2500 responses. Some of the personal food policies showed that the tribe is actually a lot wiser than food manufacturers and marketers might think. While the complete list is quite humorous and definitely worth a read (see 'Food Rules: Your Dietary Dos and Don'ts', *The New York Times*, 11 October 2009), I particularly like these three, which for me sum up the kind of food philosophy that is worth instilling in young children:

- Never eat something that is pretending to be something else.
- If you're not hungry enough to eat an apple, then you're not hungry.
- Let your kids taste everything this world has to offer – they will love and learn to eat well with gusto and with joy.

*Bon appétit!*

# INDEX

**D**
Dahlen, Hannah 12, 16–17
dairy farmers 107
dairy foods 96
Davies, Justine 16–17
daylight 82–83
deaths
  breastfeeding and 45
  SIDS 57
decision making 47
detoxification 183–84
Dettwyler, Kathy 41
developing countries 45, 78
digestive health *see* gut health
digestive system 95, 98
dips
  in lunch box 203
  recipes for kids 204–6
DNA 166, 176–77
*007 Breasts* 41
*doula* 18
dressings
  in lunch box 203
  staples for fridge 206–7
drinks 100–101

**E**
eating habits 112–17, 135
ebook readers 158–59
education 172
eggs 96, 100
egg recipes 208–9
electromagnetic radiation (EMR)
  152–54, 182
Elfman, Jenna 46
emotional health 166–67
emotional problems 157
endocrine system 82
endorphins 6–7
energy from fruit 102
'enteric' brain 47
epigenetics 166, 176–77
essential oils 28, 80
European Union 150
exercise
  for baby 123–24

for birthing 25–27
  encouraging 124–27
  as a family 127–30
explorations
  of environment 77–78
  of food 96–98
  through crawling 125–26

**F**
Facebook 159
family bed *see* co-sleeping
family exercise 127–30
family meals
  guidelines for 220–24
  introducing solid foods and 94
  nutrients in 109–10
  preparation of special meals 98
fathers *see* partners
feng shui principles 80, 82
fertility 177
first drinks 100–101
first foods 98–100
fish 100, 146
  recipes 210–11
flame-retardants 143
flexibility 130
fluorescent light 82
folic acid 179
foods
  to avoid 117
  chemicals in 181
  to eat 116–17
  first drinks 100–101
  first foods 98–99
  solid foods 93–96
  *see also* children in kitchen;
    nutrition
food allergy or intolerance 95,
  98–99, 100
food manufacturers 102
food shortages 176
food supplements 116, 178
food trauma 112–13
Foresight 175–76
formula
  breastfeeding *versus* 42, 44–45, 50

## Healthy Parents, Healthy Baby:

## A Guide to Conception & Pregnancy

### *By Jan Roberts*

'This book is for anybody who might ever become a mum or a dad
– the physical and mental health of your children is in your hands.
It all depends on your efforts before conception.
Truly beautiful, healthy, happy babies don't happen by accident!'
Jan Roberts

In simple, straightforward language Jan Roberts gives you the facts
you need to assist conception and enjoy a healthy pregnancy.

- A preconception program for you and your partner to maximise
  your fertility
- Essential information for a natural, uncomplicated, full-term
  pregnancy
- Easy tips to improve your diet, lifestyle and environment
- The truth about toxins in your home and workplace
- Quick, nutritious recipes for prospective parents and
  mums-to-be

AVAILABLE NOW